Religion, Revelation and Reason

Religion, Revelation & Reason

by Eric C. Rust

Mercer University Press
Macon, Ga. 31207

Dedication

This book is dedicated to my friend, Dr. Walter Coe, internist and cardiologist, and to Dr. Allan Lansing and his team of cardiovascular surgeons who, under God, have made possible for me a new lease on human existence.

LIBRARY OF CONGRESS CATALOGING IN PUBLICATION DATA

Rust, Eric Charles.
    Religion, revelation and reason.

    Bibliography: p.
    Includes index.
    1. Theism.   2. Philosophical theology.   I. Title.
II. Title: Religion, revelation and reason.
BT102.R87   200'.1   81-2760
ISBN 0-86554-006-3   AACR2

Table of Contents

Introduction

When I first began to teach "Philosophy of Religion" at Rawdon Baptist Theological College in England, this book began to be written. I began to shape a course which I brought across to the States and have used in its basic structure at Southern Baptist Theological Seminary in Louisville, Kentucky since 1953. With the passage of the years, fresh challenges have arisen to a rational defense of religion and of the Christian faith in particular. I have sought to deal with these, especially the challenges presented by naturalistic interpretations of science, the linguistic issues raised by the earlier and later Wittgenstein and many like thinkers, the constructions of process thought, the perennial mystery of evil and the contribution of the synthetic dimension of reason within the setting of religious experience. My treatment of the linguistic issues has not, as so often today, been given a separate chapter. Rather I have preferred to deal with its various facets as different philosophical themes have been considered.

This book begins with a general consideration of religious experience and moves to a defense of the Christian revelation as the normative one for all other divine disclosures. This means that increasingly the book moves towards a defense of theistic thought as contrasted with other religious systems. This emphasis on the approach to the understanding of God typical of the Judaeo-Christian and Islamic traditions has meant a preoccupation with issues particularly significant for this way of thinking—the nature of man, the understanding of the creative process, the problem of human survival beyond death, and the mystery of evil. I have, however, brought in the views of other religious systems and offered a critique of their relationship to the theistic position. Wherever thought has moved to the specific content of the Christian disclosure in Jesus Christ, I have stopped short. Philosophy of religion, and theistic philosophy in particular, are only prolegomena to the task of the Christian theologian.

Standing as I do in a moderating position, I have drawn on many thinkers, diverse in their own systematic thinking, yet each offering, constructively and critically, insights which have helped to illuminate my own way of thought. Footnotes and references in the course of the book will indicate many of them. I owe much to my students who across 35 years have often taught me more than I have been able to teach them. Especially is this true of those in my advanced M. Div. seminars and my Ph. D. students. As I look at the long array of bound Ph. D. dissertations upon a shelf by my desk, I realize how much I owe to men who, now in colleges, universities, seminaries and churches, have enriched my life and thought by their crucial and constructive encouragement.

The book, as with all its predecessors, would not have been written but for the support and encouragement of Helen, beloved wife and companion for 45 years. A period for open-heart surgery interrupted the final stages of the production of this book. This will explain the dedication and express my gratitude to those who have enabled me to meet the challenge of three score and ten years.

Eric C. Rust
Epiphany 1981

The Philosophical Approach
To Reality

1 Philosophy is one aspect of human reasoning. Reason is the most significant aspect of man's personal being. It is here that man differs from the animal order, although rudimentary forms of thinking can be found among the higher mammals. Such creatures manifest the presence of some degree of reasoning when confronted by an unusual situation to which the habitual responses of instinctive behavior do not apply. Rats, monkeys, chimpanzees, among others, have been found to follow a method of trial and error and to think their way through problems presented to them. But it is in man that intelligence comes to full flower, so that logical reasoning and conceptual thinking have given man a control over his environment and his own existence which lifts him to a new level of being. Aristotle defined man as a rational animal. Plato could define rationality as the supreme value in the universe. For Plato the basic reality of the universe was a rational pattern of ideas. This was reflected in the human soul in which the human reason was the central and immortal dimension.

It was the Greeks in our Western civilization who first sought to systematize man's intellectual curiosity. They used the word which became in Latin *scientia* to describe ordered and logical thinking about the various aspects of human existence. Human curiosity set out asking questions and human reason sought to supply the answers. Science was ordered reasoning pursuing the truth about some particular aspect of experience. In this use of the word science applies to every ordered discipline of rational thinking and not just to the natural sciences like physics, biology and psychology. Today the word is confined to the latter but it is better to attach the adjective 'natural' in describing them and to keep 'science' as a universal description of all ordered thinking upon human experience. Aristotle could define philosophy as "the art of arts and science of sciences," for philosophy was the pursuit of the all-embracing truth about the universe and human experience by the use of reason. We might thus define philosophy as *the rational pursuit of all-embracing, ultimate truth.*

Reason and Absolute Presuppositions

We have to be careful, however, about our use of the word 'reason'. So often we confine it to the processes of logical thinking and make it synonymous with 'reasoning'. But actually 'reason' has two dimensions—the analytic and the synthetic. The analytical dimension of reason is fundamentally associated with the logical process. Analytical reasoning works with concepts. As soon as we think, we turn the world of immediate experience into a realm of objects. We seek to universalize and identify the elements of our experience. We replace our immediate percepts and sensations by concepts and ideas which can be manipulated and given general application. Thus analytical reason takes reality to pieces and seeks to find an intelligible pattern by which these pieces can be related. It is to this area that disciplines like the natural sciences belong.

A. N. Whitehead, in his critique of scientific method, accused natural science of the fallacy of misplaced concreteness, of isolating entities and giving them a concreteness and facticity while ignoring both the whole in which they were parts and also the internality of their relations to one another. One special form of this fallacy is the fallacy of simple location. In the process of isolating, physical science divides its world into lumps of matter separated in space and moving in time to such a degree that it has to relate them externally by the idea of causation. Thereby science ignores the inner relatedness in which entities spill over their spatio-temporal frontiers and are intimately and internally related to one another. The mechanical relationship of causation replaces the unity which primarily pervades the natural order.

This tendency to isolate and separate indicates the abstract nature of analytical reasoning. As soon as we seek to conceptualize our world and represent it to ourselves as a world of detached objects, we have to relate them again in order to match the continuity present in our immediate experience. The more we conceptualize and order our world in this way the more abstract it becomes, and the more removed it is from the concreteness and wholeness of the world of which we are immediately aware.

Leaving on one side Whitehead's own characteristic philosophy, he has reminded us that there is another dimension of reason in which an intuitive feeling for wholeness is predominant. This synthetic aspect of reason is one in which the mind is immediately aware of wholes. Indeed we are only concerned to analyze the parts and relate them, because we have this prior awareness of wholeness. Michael Polanyi has called it the tacit dimension of knowing and points out that it is a significant aspect of all our awareness of our world. Indeed natural science and the other rational disciplines could not function without it. Natural science goes searching for a solution to a problem because the scientist already is tacitly aware of a pattern of wholeness which he hopes to establish by his analytical reasoning and investigation. Polanyi suggests, therefore, that all our knowledge is personal knowledge in the sense that all our rational investigations of experience involve a prior commitment to a pattern of wholeness which we believe to be present.

This emphasis is especially significant when we come to philosophy. For philosophy is *the attempt of reason to establish the overall rational pattern which makes intelligible the whole universe and the whole of human experience.* It seeks for some underlying principle which makes our world understandable. Of course every science is doing something of the same thing within the limits of its own discipline. The difference is that the philosopher is endeavoring to find a unifying and connecting principle which brings together and makes intelligible the many areas of human experience with which the specific sciences and rational disciplines respectively deal.

This does not mean that philosophy simply sums up the findings of these various disciplines and coordinates their conclusions. It is no mere catalogue of the separate results of the various sciences (in the broad sense of ordered investigations). Rather it seeks rationally for an underlying and unifying principle which will bring together in one intelligible whole the results of the investigations of the varied dimensions of human experience. It seeks to transcend all the natural and human sciences and all the areas covered by the humanities in such a way that it unifies the whole of experience by one integrating and connecting principle. It looks for wholeness and moves beyond the abstraction to which the analytical reason is prone. It looks for an organic wholeness and connecting purpose which illuminates all human experience.

This means that the material of philosophy covers the whole realm of nature and history, every facet of human experience. The material studied by the natural sciences, by the human and social sciences, by the arts and human history, by the normative sciences, like ethics and aesthetics, and by religious theologies is all grist for the mill. The so-called facts of nature and history and the values which are expressed in human life and historical experience all provide its data. It must and does take note of what the various disciplines and rationally directed studies may find in their investigations. Yet it must go beyond this and find a principle which makes sense of the findings of all these investigations and which brings the universe together in one organic pattern of wholeness. It can never fall into the method of the individual described by Charles Dickens. This person was asked to write an article on "Chinese metaphysics." He did so by consulting, in the *Encyclopaedia Britannica*, the respective articles on China and metaphysics and putting them together.

Now in looking for such a unifying principle, the philosopher, like the natural scientist, is driven by a heuristic passion which is grounded in a tacit awareness of some underlying wholeness. We only ask questions because we are tacitly aware of an answer. The philosopher is committed, as are all thinkers, to a belief in the power of human reasoning, but this involves the acceptance of the validity of felt intuitive insights which color the movement of his thought. Behind his analytical reasoning lies his synthetic reason, his intuitive insight into the nature of reality which lures him on to investigate with heuristic passion.

At no level does thinking begin without a selection of what is significant in the data under consideration. What we believe to be significant is not, however, the result of logical argument. Rather it is the ground of such argument. The judgment of significance results from an intuitive feeling which springs out of our experience of our world or out of a conviction which the pressure of human existence forces upon us. It is this synthetic insight, this holistic judgment, which underlies our thinking. The processes of human reasoning have behind them an absolute presupposition in which our judgment of significance is enshrined. This is true of all thinking and in particular of philosophical thinking. Every philosopher gathers his data around some aspect of experience which for him has become central in his understanding of the world. This focal point provides the absolute presupposition of his rational investigation of human experience of the world. We could also call this a faith hypothesis, for it is the hypothetical starting point of his thought to which he is committed as the key to the meaning of his world. This is, indeed, the world-view, the *Weltanschauung*, which characterizes his understanding of reality.

Such a philosophical absolute presupposition provides the philosopher with a model which becomes basic in his understanding of his world. This model illuminates for him every aspect of human experience. It is, indeed, a model for ultimate reality. Just as the natural scientist seeks for a model to help him understand some mysterious data in his investigation, so the philosopher seeks for one which provides a key for understanding the mysterious depths of his world. In the sciences, the models are analogies provided by some other phenomenon which the sciences have come to understand. Thus the solar system initially provided a basic model for understanding the mysterious structure of the atom. The electrons whirled around the nucleus of the atom like the planets around the sun. Again, two models came to be keys for understanding the mysterious behavior of the electron—sometimes it was best understood as a wave and at other times a particle. As someone has said: "On Mondays, Wednesdays and Fridays, it behaves like a particle. On Tuesdays, Thursdays, and Saturdays, it behaves like a wave. And on Sundays you pray about it for you are not quite sure what it is." In the same way, philosophy finds its absolute presuppositions and their accompanying models in the familiar areas of human experience and seeks to penetrate with them into the mysterious depths of reality.

Models are thus analogies. As such they must not be taken too literally. For there are aspects of their original sources which do not apply in their new use. What they do is to enable the philosopher to penetrate more deeply into the ultimate meaning of the universe and to integrate better the manifold human experiences of the world.

Philosophical Models and Systems

In philosophical thought, history has produced a multiplicity of systems of thought, each characterized by an absolute presupposition with its accompanying model. Any understanding of what philosophy is about requires an understanding of such systems and also of the vocabulary which is employed.

Every system involves the issue of 'epistemology'. The term designates the nature of knowing. It is concerned with how and what we know. Do we know only through sense experience and the logical processes operating upon such data? Or are there other ways of knowing and is more involved than just reason operating upon sense data? In the first case, systems which operate under this premise about 'knowing' are labelled 'empiricist'. Any form of empiricism is tied to the knowledge available through sense-experience. In the second case, systems which operate with the conviction that the experiences associated with moral, aesthetic and religious value judgments and with awareness of other persons are valid ways of knowing. Often such systems accept the validity of the intuitive or synthetic dimension of reason, although as we have suggested this is universally present whether we acknowledge it or not.

Logical reasoning has a significant place in all systems whatever their basic approach to the knowing process. Such rational thinking involves both inductive logic and deductive logic. Inductive logic moves from the multiplicity of sense data to the discovery of some general underlying principle which links such data together and makes them intelligible. It is therefore an important aspect of scientific method for, ever since they began, the natural sciences have sought for laws which describe the relationships between the various phenomena which they study. On the other hand, deductive logic is the movement from some general proposition to its logical consequences. It therefore involves a certainty which is not present in inductive logic. The conclusions arrived at in the latter are no more certain than the number of individual cases from which the generalizations are derived. The larger the number of individual data, the higher the probability of the conclusion being valid. With deductive logic, however, the certainty of the conclusions turns upon the certainty of the proposition which provides the starting point of the logical process. If this proposition is clearly self-evident or universal in its application then a conclusion deduced from it will be equally valid. An outstanding example of such deductive logic is the science of mathematics. We have only to think of Euclid's geometry with its axioms to remind ourselves of this.

Granted the presence of such logical procedures, every philosophical system is rationally valid within the limits set by its absolute presupposition with the accompanying model of reality. This means that there is a plurality of interpretations of the universe, depending upon what the thinker believes to be the key for understanding the ultimate reality which underlies the world of his experience. Within the logical development of any system the thinker may assert his claims for truth. Everything will turn upon the premise with which he starts. When two thinkers are arguing from different and even opposed starting points, absolute presuppositions or faith-hypotheses that clash, they are not likely to reach much agreement. Indeed, to understand why any thinker argues as he does we must find out what it is to which he is in truth committed. *Men think as they do because they believe as they do.*

Sidney Smith, the English Regency wit and clergyman of the early 1800's, was on one occasion walking to St. Paul's cathedral, of which he was a canon, and proceeding along one of the very narrow streets which surrounded the cathedral in those days. The street was so narrow that the second floors of some houses on opposite sides leaned out of the vertical and almost touched. He saw two women arguing across the street from two such opposite windows. His witty comment drives home our point: "Those two women will never agree for they are arguing from different premises."

The plurality of philosophical systems arises from the manifold nature of human experience. Persons live in relation to nature and to other persons. They function as they do because they enjoy a mental and reflective life as well as bodily existence. They are subject to moral obligations, aesthetic visions, and religious convictions. But they are also intimately bound up with the realm of nature and its scientific investigation. Technological achievements and the findings of the natural sciences impress themselves upon modern man because of their evident success in controlling his environment. The mental sciences such as psychology have burgeoned in our time to such a degree that modern man tends to accept their gospel as authoritative despite the fact that there are as many psychologies as there are views of man. All this affects human judgments of significance and leads increasingly to differing convictions as to the nature of ultimate reality.

So we may broadly classify the systems as naturalistic/materialistic, idealistic, dualistic, and personalist. The purely materialistic philosophies hold that physical matter is the sole reality and that all other aspects of the world from life through personal being and mind can be explained as complex rearrangements of the physical stuff. It is difficult to identify any such systems nowadays, since naturalistic philosophies have taken over. Building upon an empirical view of knowledge and accepting the scientific approach to nature, such thinkers believe that nature is the sole reality and that its natural forces underlie and explain all man's experience. Thus naturalism reduces human mental experience to psychological conditioning, so that man's thinking is determined by his cultural environment. We find this in the thought of B. F. Skinner. Moral experience is reduced to the level of behavior which has survival value. Ethical values have no eternal and unchanging significance. Rather they describe behavior which best enables the human race to survive in the process of time. Moral obligation is simply the result of group pressure. As for religious experience, that arises because man seeks to escape from the frustrations and alienations of existence by projecting a portrait of his ideal self and of the ideal human situation upon the backdrop of the universe and labeling them God and heaven respectively. This approach was first propounded in modern times by Feuerbach and has been reformulated in various ways by Freud and Marx. Naturalism is thus closely associated with both the natural and mental sciences and with a reductionist approach to reality. Nature and its forces are all that is.

A term closely parallel in meaning to naturalism is 'positivism'. First coined by the French thinker Auguste Comte, this label describes any system of thought which rejects all speculation that takes the thinker beyond what is scientifically observable. Hence any attempt to develop a metaphysical system and establish a reality which transcends what can be observed by sense experience is rejected. Empiricism is the only way of knowing and the scientific approach to reality is regnant. All that a philosopher may do is describe reality as the scientific disciplines have made it known. Any speculative thinking which moves beyond this and seeks for some explanation which transcends what can be empirically established is invalid. Propositions grounded in spiritual experiences are non-sensical. They do not make sense because they are not empirically grounded. The current form of positivism is 'logical positivism', which examines propositional statements and rejects as non-sensical all which cannot be validated or falsified at the empirical level. Its exponents are thinkers like the early Wittgenstein, Carnap, A. J. Ayers, Gilbert Ryle and others.

Such approaches to reality can hardly lay claim to the titles 'metaphysics' or 'ontologies' as do the other systems of philosophical thought. It is now time to define these terms. 'Metaphysics' was originally coined by Aristotle to describe the volume of his philosophical thinking which followed his volume on nature. Literally it means 'beyond nature'. It is used to describe attempts to find and express the ultimate reality which underlies the whole universe. Such attempts seek to penetrate behind the natural to those mysterious depths of the universe to which moral, aesthetic and religious experience and the nature of human personality bear testimony. Ignoring naturalistic reductionism, such systems endeavor to establish the validity of man's ideal value judgments and to show that they point to an underlying reality or principle which makes possible an intelligible understanding of all experience.

'Ontology' is, in one sense, a parallel term to metaphysics, but it is especially concerned with the study of 'being', a term which is of common occurrence in philosophical thinking. 'Being', in the original Greek, stood for 'what is'. It stands in contrast to becoming and thus it indicates what endures through change in contrast to the development and change which are so evident in our sense experience of the world and its things. Thus the being of a thing is its essence, its essential meaning. Ontology is, however, not just a search for the essences which lie behind and within the individual phenomena of sense experience. At this level it would be described as 'phenomenology'.

Essences are universals and linguistically are the concepts with which logical discourse is concerned. They are common to all individual phenomena of the same type. Ontology, however, moves beyond this. It is concerned with 'being itself', as some philosophers describe it, the unchanging substratum of all existent beings, the enduring principle or ultimate reality which sustains and gives meaning to all such existents. In this sense, philosophy is the search for Being and a logical validation of what it believes Being to be.

Now our experience of the world brings us face to face with both Being and Becoming, and philosophers have, ever since the beginning of philosophical thought, believed that ultimate reality is either an unchanging substratum of Being or that the ultimate truth of the universe lies in change and becoming. Both positions present problems, as two Greek thinkers soon discovered—Parmenides who believed that change was an illusion and Heraclitus who believed that everything flows. In our own time we have philosophers like Bergson and Croce who, each in his own distinctive approach, have sought to develop philosophical systems which presuppose change as the significant dimension in reality. Plato and, still more, Aristotle both launched philosophical systems in which change and becoming had their place within an ultimate reality of static being. In this modern period the emphasis upon evolution and dynamic energy in the natural sciences has pointed to the necessity of philosophical systems which have a place for becoming in some way within being itself, if ontological thinking is to survive as a viable discipline.

Not only does sense experience present the contrast of being and becoming, but it also points to the presence of another contrast—the one and the many. This also plays a part in the formulation of those judgments of significance which we have described as absolute presuppositions or faith-hypotheses. The atomic theory has become instrumental in the tendency to emphasize the many, but the organic dimension of the biological sciences has pointed to the tendency to unify and thus to emphasize the one. Systems can be classified as monistic or pluralistic according as their authors believe that ultimate reality is one or many. We need to note that pluralistic systems always manifest a strong urge to find some principle which binds the many together, while monistic systems rarely ignore the reality of the many, whatever degree of reality they may give to individual entities. We shall see this immediately illustrated in the more detailed consideration of systems to which we now turn.

In our experience it is quite clear that the human mind plays a leading role. Indeed, even those who emphasize the physical and major upon man's bodily aspect could not think or develop such a system which denies reality to mind without possessing a mind themselves. This is, of course, the ridiculous situation in which we humans find ourselves. We devise denials of that very dimension of our being without which no human thought would be possible. Those thinkers whose judgment of significance emphasizes mind in its many functions and who regard the physical order as derivative and actually an appearance of what is basically mental are labelled 'idealists'. We need to remember that this term is used quite differently in popular speech. There it describes a person who is so concerned with ideals, perfect objectives and almost unattainable dreams, that he often fails to be realistic. In philosophy, however, the emphasis falls, not on such ideals, but on 'ideas', the conceptual structures in the mind which are basic in the thought processes.

The first idealist to stand out in human thinking was Plato, and ever since there has been a perennial stream of such thought. To it belong outstanding figures like Aristotle, Augustine, Aquinas, Leibnitz, Berkeley, Kant and Hegel. The simplest illustration of what such thinking involves is the system devised by Berkeley, although we need to remember that the model of the universe which he offered was far too simplistic for acceptance by other idealistic thinkers. Berkeley was also an empiricist, a reminder that empiricists are not necessarily naturalistic or positivistic! He believed that all knowledge comes through the senses. Hence, since as an idealist he believed that the mind and its ideas were basic to reality, he held that 'being' is 'perceiving'. This meant that the 'ideas' or concepts in the mind were received through the senses. But then when a thing was not being perceived, it would not exist. For its 'being' depended upon its being perceived. To resolve his dilemma, Berkeley brought in God as the supreme mind which was always thinking the 'ideas' and presenting them to us through our sensorium. Then 'matter' is the result of the objective appearance of the 'ideas' which are presented to us. The material world is dissolved into the objective appearance of the mental, and reality becomes 'Mind'. A limerick has expressed this very cleverly:

> There was a young man who said: "God
> Must think it exceedingly odd
>> That the form of that tree
>> Continues to be
> When there's no one about in the quad."

The answer:

> "Dear Sir, your astonishment's odd,
> For I'm always about in the quad,
>> And the form of that tree
>> Will continue to be
> Since observed by yours faithfully, God."

Other forms of idealism, and much more acceptable ones, also involve, in their absolute presuppositions, monistic or pluralistic premises. Berkeley had basically assumed a theistic approach to reality, that is to say, he assumed the reality of a God as creator and a number of created minds possessing their own degree of independent being. Hegel, on the other hand, had, as a basic concept, a belief in one mind which, for the purpose of self-realization, distributed itself in a number of minds as its subjective centers and in the processes of nature and society as their objective counterparts. Thus the universe becomes a vast dialectical movement of logical development and again the physical is only the objectification, the objective appearance, of the mental. Reality is mind and its ideas.

Leibnitz, on the other hand, opted for the many. For him also, the material world was dissolved into a mental reality and its atomic multiplicity was transformed in mental entities at various levels of mentality, unconscious and conscious. Their physical relationships, such as spatial, temporal and causative, were appearances of their mental nature. The whole universe was thus built up of a vast array of such 'monads', as Leibnitz called them. Then a human being would be a colony of monads, the body being an aggregate of monads at lower levels of mental responsiveness, and the soul being the key monad of the structure at the full level of self-consciousness. It is interesting to note that Leibnitz, who was a pioneer in many areas, was the first to speak about 'unconscious' mind, a concept now commonly accepted. Leibnitz found, as do all such thinkers, that the many without some unifying principle, a one, become chaotic. So he moved to a theistic position and postulated a creator God. But he did not, like Hegel, regard the many as logical differentiations of the one Mind. His many were created by God 'out of nothing', the classical position of theism.

At this juncture we shall need to return to the issue of *Epistemology*, the investigation of how and what we know. In moving from naturalism to idealism this issue is raised in an acute form. The world which we know through sense experience, the world of the empiricist, has the form of a solid, physical, material structure. An empiricist or naturalist would generally adopt a realist stance and hold that this world is as it appears to him, although he might modify such a stance by acknowledging that sense experience may contribute the secondary qualities of color, taste and smell for example. But the primary sense qualities of location in space, motion in time, and the derived assumption of solidity and substance really belong to the world. They are objective. Yet even the scientist would contend, at least when it comes to the microscopic order of atomic particles, that there is a large degree of imagination and of subjectively devised structures involved.

When we turn to idealism, as we have just seen, the objective physical realm is dissolved into 'appearance'. The term 'phenomena' is employed to describe the world as it appears to us in sense experience. Thus, for the idealist, reality is actually mental in structure. It is akin to mind, even though the phenomenal world of sense experience assumes a physical form. This form is the result of the objectifying process which is a part of sense perception.

The modern thinker who clearly elaborated this was Immanuel Kant, and we shall later examine the challenging way in which he developed his critical idealism. It was challenging because it decisively changed the development of philosophical thought and did for philosophy what Copernicus did for science. Kant held that the mind possesses certain inherent structures through which sense experience passes and is shaped in order that it may become the object of knowledge, attain objectification. Thus, in empirical knowledge, we never know the thing in itself but only its appearance. What it is, its *noumenal* reality, is not known. Only the *phenomenal* reality is grasped by sense experience. We know only appearance empirically. Hence Kant had to find another way of grasping reality itself, being, the noumenal.

As this book develops, we shall look at dualists who do not reduce mind to physical forces as do many naturalists nor dissolve the physical reality by regarding it as an appearance of mind. Rather they postulate two principles in the universe—matter and mind, entirely distinct and yet somehow bound together. The outstanding example of this highly questionable way of thinking is Descartes.

Much more important is the personalistic way of philosophizing. Here the absolute presupposition is that ultimate reality is personal and thus the basic model is 'personal being'. We shall not develop this further at this point, since it is the way in which the thought of this book will move. It is important, however, to note that aspects of the idealistic position are retained but the dimensions of freedom, feeling and willing in human personality find a significant place alongside man's rational structures. In our discussion we also shall examine in detail the contribution of existentialist philosophies, which insofar as they develop into ontology, are best included within the broad label of personalist philosophies.

Philosophy of Religion and its Presuppositions

We turn now to examine philosophically one area of human experience, the religious dimension of the human psyche. Behind such an investigation there lies the question about the implications of such experience when it is taken as the focal point for understanding the nature of ultimate reality and as the integrating center for unifying all man's experience of his world. This consideration will therefore fall into two parts—a phenomenological investigation of the nature of religion and an ontological consideration of the validity of religious experience for providing a viable model of reality.

At the phenomenological level, we are concerned with the nature of the religious consciousness and how valid it is as a way of knowing compared with the empirical approach to the universe. In doing so we must ask how far knowledge of the supra-sensible is possible and how such knowledge differs from our knowledge of the secular. Furthermore, we must inquire into the objective counterpart of religious knowledge, the nature of the revelation which the religious consciousness claims to possess and which makes religious knowledge possible. This involves the consideration of the various and differing claims which the religious consciousness makes regarding knowledge of the supra-sensible—the variety of religions.

At the ontological level, we shall turn our attention to the way in which this variety of claims leads to various metaphysical systems. In such systems the absolute presupposition is a religious one. The model for ultimate reality involved will depend upon the specific nature of the revelation to which the religious consciousness involved lays claim. This means that there are many differing religious views of the world. Since each such view will claim to provide an adequate and valid understanding of the universe in every facet of human experience of it, the truth claims of such views have to be considered, and the issue of truth lifts its head.

The place of reason in religious experience is thus of supreme importance. Constructive and critical rational processes are a necessary part of any adequate consideration of the religious consciousness when it lays claim to knowledge of supra-sensible reality and of deity. Each system will have its own specific claim to such knowledge and also accompanying beliefs about the nature of man and the world. Knowledge of God, man, the world are all within the purview of any religious philosophy and such knowledge must be made rationally viable. Thus each system will have to be considered in its implications with regard to the nature of deity; to the issue of divine transcendence and immanence; to the relationship of the world to the deity as creation, independence, and so forth; to the nature of man including the problem of immortality; to the mystery of evil and its place in a religious view of the universe. This means that the religious beliefs of each system have to be analyzed and criticized as to their adequacy and viability in the light of the knowledge of our world which other disciplines supply, especially the findings of the natural sciences, the mental sciences, and historical investigations. The religious system which we accept has to be defended as offering the most viable rational understanding of reality.

The various religious metaphysic systems are defined in the light of their understanding of the relation of God and the world. At this stage, such definitions are in order, so that the descriptive labels can be identified as the investigation proceeds. Two terms need immediately to be defined—immanence and transcendence. Here we shall make no attempt to seek models that facilitate our understanding. These will be developed much later. Here it is sufficient that divine immanence describes the presence of the deity in the world whereas divine transcendence describes the beyondness of deity to and otherness of deity from the world. The words 'presence', 'beyondness', and 'otherness' will be more carefully defined later in our discussion.

The first religious system to be considered majors on the immanence of deity and regards deity as the sole reality. It identifies everything else, the world and man, as in some way or other a manifestation of the divine. It is called *pantheism*, and it takes two forms. *Cosmic pantheism* identifies the world in its totality with God so that universe is itself divine. Here God is not necessarily or even visually pictured on the pattern of a personal model. Deity is usually impersonal or supra-personal, whatever this latter nomenclature may indicate. We might say that pantheism identifies God with the All, and that in this form the emphasis falls on the world as the All. God is all that is, and the world is divine. Insofar as naturalism ever develops religious pretensions, and sometimes it does, it would take this form. Here there is no thought of creation, since the world is itself divine, and religious experience tends to be mystical. Men recognize their own divinity and seek mystical absorption in the deity which is present in and identified with their own being. As well as religious forms of naturalism, Spinoza's philosophy affords a good example of this kind of system at the rational level, and Greek Stoicism has strong affinities with it.

The other form of pantheism is *acosmic pantheism*. In this approach to reality, only the soul of man is real and the world is illusory. Hence God is identified with the human soul, and man's religious experience is concerned with recognition of his own identification with and absorption in God. Again, mysticism is the characteristic form of religious experience. The emphasis is on God— the All is God, and the world is illusion. Hinduism in its basic and classical form is the outstanding illustration of this religious approach to reality.

At the other extreme to pantheism, with its exclusive emphasis on the divine immanence, is *deism* with its exclusive emphasis on the divine transcendence. A personal model for God is usually basic. The deity is regarded as totally other and beyond the world, which moves along lines that are set by its own innate tendencies. God's relation to the world is that of creator, but otherwise he does not intervene in its process. He leaves it to move according to the laws and energies which he built into it in the act of creation. Man's religious experience becomes much more a rational and moral act than an emotional feeling. In actual fact, to speak of such deism is much like setting up a straw man, for it is difficult to find any system which purely manifests such an extreme emphasis on transcendence. Probably Aristotle's philosophy comes nearest. In the period of the Enlightenment, we find the historical deists who include our own founding fathers such as Franklin, John Adams and Thomas Jefferson, the French Encyclopedists such as Voltaire and Diderot, and English thinkers like Locke and Hume. Yet, in varying degrees, none completely separated the deity from the world. While ruling out miraculous intervention, they still allowed for a sustaining and ruling presence. Religion certainly for them took the form of moral behavior and rational speculation. Islam also presents a good example of a religious approach to reality which emphasizes transcendence, yet with modifications. Its emphasis on law and on kismet points to a deity who is transcendent and majestically regnant. Yet its sufi mysticism and sayings in the Koran such as Allah being nearer to a man than his own neck-vein are indications that the divine immanence is also a reality in Moslem thought.

Between the extremes of pantheism and deism, we find *panentheism* and classical *theism*. The latter is a special form of the former. Panentheism, as its name implies, is the world-view which regards the universe as all in God without totally identifying God with it. In its characteristic form, therefore, it thinks of the deity as both immanent in the world and also transcendent to it. The world and men live and move and have their being within God, but he transcends them. They come into being by a divine act of creation, but the deity shapes them out of the divine substance, so that they are themselves derivative from the divine being and manifestations of that being. In some forms of panentheism the derivation of finite beings from the divine being is not by such a voluntary creative act, but through an involuntary emergence from the divine being. The deity is so superabundant, to speak figuratively, that it spills over. Since the world and men are derived from the divine being but also finite structures of being, they, in both forms, manifest imperfection because of their finitude. Yet fundamentally they have the divine spark deep down in their own being. Here the divine may be pictured in terms of a personal model or may be described as supra-personal. The aspect of transcendence is retained. The creatures participate in deity, but deity transcends them. Hence religion is usually concerned with mystery and religious experience often takes a mystical form.

An outstanding example of the involuntary form of derivation of the finite order of being is Neo-Platonism. Here the many emerge from the one and participate in it, despite the imperfections implicit in their finitude. Their religious experience is focalized in mystical contemplation and thereby they return to the One from which they are derived. The voluntary form of derivation can be illustrated from many thinkers, including Paul Tillich as we shall see later. Perhaps, however, we might refer to Hegel who thinks of all creatures as having adjectival existence. They are finite manifestations of the Absolute Rational Spirit which realizes itself in the logical dialectic that they make possible. Here religious experience is secondary to the rational dialectic, for the Absolute Spirit is rational mind, impersonal rather than personal.

Classical theism is similar to panentheism and might be described as a special form of it. It is especially related to the Jewish and Christian approach to the world. Its model for God is personal, and it regards God as both transcendent to and immanent in the world which he has created. It can speak of the world and its constituent creatures as living, moving, and having their being in God. Yet the divine act of creation is one which posits the world and men over against God. They are created 'out of nothing'. This phrase is an attempt to exclude any thought of divine substance in the created order. The latter results from an act or acts of the divine will, but, although it derives from that act, it is not derived from the divine being, the divine substance. Its being is posited over nothing by the divine act. It is totally dependent upon the divine activity, but it does not share in the divine being. It is truly a creature. Furthermore, it is possible for God to intervene specially within the ordered structure which he has created and sustains. Men are not possessors of a divine spark or essentially divine. They are creatures who may enjoy fellowship with God, and communion becomes central in the religious response. Mysticism can no longer take the form of absorption. When present its basis is communion.

The Two Religious Approaches to Ultimate Reality

Paul Tillich has emphasized the two different approaches to

ultimate reality which are evident in the various religious philosophies, especially in cosmic pantheism, panentheism and classical theism. He describes them respectively as ontological and cosmological and contends that both are necessary in an all-embracing attempt to express a religious philosophy. He rightly holds that the cosmological without the ontological leads to a cleavage between the secular and the religious realms.

The word 'ontological' is unfortunately subject to diverse interpretations, although, as we have already indicated, it is concerned with the pursuit of the ground of all being, being itself, the ultimate principle which underlies all that is, all beings. The ontological method in religious philosophizing has this basic concern, but it is further defined by our initial experiential preoccupation with personal self-awareness and its relation to consciousness of the Other. In self-consciousness there is an immediate awareness of the self but this is bound up with an immediate awareness of the Ground of such personal being. Furthermore the ontological approach contends that such awareness is the *prius* of the subject/object antithesis in which all knowing is involved. Being (capitalized) is thus thought with every being. Indeed, it is the ground of all beings, since without Being there would be no beings at all. At this point, in modern philosophical thought, ontological thinking links on to *existentialism*.

The latter like the ontological approach goes back to St. Augustine, but more immediately its leading exponents have been Pascal and Kierkegaard with atheistic counterparts like Nietzsche and Sartre. Heidegger, Tillich and Macquarrie have demonstrated how closely existentialist thinking moves into ontological developments. In existentialism, the emphasis falls on the will and human decision. Face to face with the issues of human life, man has to decide his 'existence', and here 'existence' means "life which possesses meaning." 'Existence' is meaningful existence, what an individual decides about his way of living. Thus existentialism is the search of man for self-understanding. The religious existentialist contends that 'existence' (in this sense) is authentic when it is decided in the light of awareness of God, the ground of being. The non-religious existentialist is still concerned with Being, although he may identify it with Not-Being or Nothing. It is thus easy to move into ontological thinking.

In this approach to ultimate reality, reason occupies a central place, but the emphasis tends to fall primarily on will, on personal being and self-awareness, on religious experience rather than on rational speculation. The latter characterizes the second method in religious philosophy—the cosmological. Such thinking, as its name implies, begins with the objective world of nature rather than the subjective world of personal selfhood. It is almost inevitable that our thinking should be bifurcated in these ways, since all our knowledge falls into the subject/object antithesis. The history of philosophical thinking shows the way in which the emphasis has varied in different thinkers between the knowing, feeling mind and world which is the object of knowledge.

We have already suggested, however, that such an antithesis can only be a valid source of knowledge if Being provides its *prius*, its ground. Thus if the way of cosmological speculation from the objective world is to be valid, the convictions embodied in the ontological approach are a necessary accompaniment. For, if philosophy is the search for the Truth, there must be an underlying Ground which unites subject and object because it is itself the Truth. The very awareness of this reality of Being is the basis of any speculative pursuit of truth. God who is the Truth is the presupposition of all speculation which endeavors to establish the reality of God. God can never be turned into an object without ceasing to be God, for he is the Ground which unites every subject to every object and makes knowledge possible.

Once we grant this, the development of religious philosophy along the cosmological line is best described as *natural theology*, the attempt of the unaided reason to establish the reality and nature of God on the basis of man's knowledge of his world. Such natural theology is of value as giving reasons for holding religious convictions, but it only establishes rationally that which is the presupposition of all knowledge, that reason can attain the Truth. And reason can attain the truth, because the living Truth is the basis of all our knowing and of all our rational preoccupation with the subject/object dichotomy of human existence.

We shall find as we proceed that each of these approaches develops its own form of argument—the ontological and cosmological/ teleological respectively. For each, as a philosophy, is concerned with rational validation and development. Actually both demonstrate the initial affirmation of this chapter that discussive reason always leans back upon an absolute presupposition or faith-hypothesis without which it could not operate selectively within the multitudinous data provided by human experience.

The Religious Response
To Reality

2 If we are to develop a religious philosophy, we must begin with
   a phenomenological investigation of the religious response to
   reality. Because man's religions are so diverse, we
must seek to understand what this religious response always involves
and not concentrate upon any specific characteristics which are peculiar
to only one or to a small group of the religions of mankind. Thus
phenomenologically we have to concern ourselves with what generally
characterizes the religious response to reality and what distinguishes it
from other responses. This, however, will involve us in the
epistemological issue. How far does the religious response offer valid
knowledge and what is the nature of revelation to which all religions lay
some claim?

The Psychological Dimensions of the Religious Consciousness

Insofar as modern psychology has helped us to understand the
workings and functions of the human mind, we must take note of the
data which it provides. Such data are concerned with human behavior in
religious situations and must be seriously considered in any attempt to
define the nature of the religious consciousness. We have long since
realized that the human consciousness acts as a unity and that the
various elements which constitute it all function in its approach to any
situation. Thus religious consciousness cannot be regarded as associated
with an aspect of the human consciousness which functions in its case

and in no other. The human consciousness cannot be pictured as an assembly of limbs which function only when a specific situation requires it. Such an idea of the mind possessing a distinctive religious faculty which operates only in a religious situation has long since been left behind. We know that the same mental 'stuff' is present in every activity of the human consciousness and that what is distinctive in the religious consciousness must lie in the effect of a religious object upon the various aspects of the human mental response. Always that mental response manifests an affective or emotive aspect, a cognitive aspect, and a conative or behavioral aspect. Feeling, thought (reflective and imaginative), impulse to act (voluntary or involuntary) all find their place in our response to any situation. What distinguishes any particular response depends upon that which evokes it, and it is at this point that religious thinkers face the issue of validation. For there have always been those who have endeavored to reduce the religious response to the level of the more mundane and secular and to dismiss what appears to be a distinctive element in it as illusory, a subjective product of the human imagination.

An illustration of this last device is seen in the association of religion with fear which occurred quite early in philosophical thinking. It was and still remains fairly easy to identify religion with superstition and to emphasize the element of fear as characteristic of the religious response to the world. Thus Lucretius and the Epicurean philosophers regarded religion as basically superstition, and Petronius could write: *primus in orbe deos facit timor.* In more modern times, we find Hume likewise ascribing religious behavior to the motivation of fear. He does, however, modify this by admitting hope as another factor. Hobbes likewise affirmed that the natural seed of religion lay in devotion towards what men fear.

A careful consideration of the data available from the manifold forms of religious experience shows that fear is a constituent element of the emotional side of religion but that it is usually mingled with love, gratitude, devotion and wonder to form the complex emotion of awe or godly fear. For religions usually display a mixture of fear and fascination, of repulsion and attraction. Otto makes much of this, as we shall see later. There is, however, also present a feeling of dependence and sometimes a feeling of ecstasy and rapture. We think immediately of the religious dances of American Indians and African Negroes as illustrations of the latter.

Yet feeling never makes up the totality of religious experience. It is always a feelingful awareness of a mysterious presence. It has an intuitive dimension. It has an objective reference and thus involves, however vaguely, some attempt at ideation. All religions have an inherent element of cognition and belief, even at the most primitive level. At this basic level, pictorial thinking is central. Indeed religion can never escape the language of myth and symbol, however much more developed theologies may endeavor to express their religious truths in more rational and logical form. Creative imagination early gets to work, in order to give content to the religious feeling of that mysterious and divine presence by which the feeling has been evoked. Myth and symbol endeavor to express that feelingful awareness in terms of the more familiar experience of mundane things and human persons. The deity or deities are pictured in concrete images borrowed from everyday life. Stories are told of them which portray their experienced activity in a way which reflects the more familiar activity of human life. So myth and symbol arise as the creative imagination molds the feelingful awareness of the supernatural Presence into communicable form. Such poetic and pictorial thinking is natural to religious experience, and even in the advanced religions like Christianity this aspect remains. There is a personal, concrete aspect to the religious experience of the divine presence which is lost in rational abstraction.

Yet thought and activity are closely interrelated in religion. Indeed Marett has contended that, at the primitive level, religion was more danced out than thought out. It is certainly true that religious myth and ritual are closely intertwined, and that religious activity is closely bound up with the mythical and symbolic forms in which religious belief is expressed. If we ask what human behavior is associated especially with religious experience, we might divide it up into activity directed specifically to the deity and activity concerned with human relationships.

The first group of activities would embrace public worship and private devotion and would include prayers and sacrifices. The paraphernalia of institutional religion centers in the two latter activities throughout the long history of man's religious development and throughout the catalogue of his many religions. In the early days of man's historical development, sacrifices took many forms, and often included human sacrifices. Two characteristic modes of animal sacrifice are evident. In one, the whole animal is offered up on the altar and consumed by fire as a homage to the god. In the other, the entrails and so forth are separated from the flesh, and the whole is shared with the deity in a sacrificial communal meal. The latter was common among the Semites and was known among the Hebrews as a communion-meal or peace-meal offering. Special manipulation of the blood was associated with the idea that it carried the life-principle and was sacred to deity. Prayers were apparently closely identified with magical spells in the early days, for it is evident that magic and religion developed side by side. They diverged as religion's emphasis on a mysterious Presence produced, in antithesis, the belief that man could constrain by magic the mysterious powers of the universe to serve his purpose. Prayer as humble persuasion and devout petition diverged from spell as magical constraint. Elements of the magical approach still linger in religious practice even today.

The second group of activities embraces man's moral behavior. Quite early, man's social mores were put under the direction of the deity. Some religious anthropologists would say that this was so from the very beginning. It is certainly true that morality and religion have been bound together in the major part of religious development. All the world's major religions have a significant ethical dimension in their religious requirements. As tribal morals were early under the guardianships of the deity, so man's ethical behavior forms an important part of his religious activity in both the historical religions of Judaism, Islam and Christianity, and the mystical and world-denying religions like Hinduism and Buddhism.

As a consequence of this duality of behavior, religion has always had a tendency to follow two lines of development. It has thus produced a sacramental stream, with its accompanying sacerdotalism, and a moral stream which has been concerned with bringing all life under the discipline of religious duty. We find the priest and his ceremonial concerns over against the prophet with his ethical demands and judgments. The right performance of ritual stands in contrast to righteous conduct. Both are claimed to be in the service of the deity.

Religion as Moral Behavior or as Rational Speculation

Because the conative and cognitive aspects of religion loom large in later developments there has always been a tendency to regard religion as a peculiar manifestation of man's moral experience, or else to regard it as a very immature form of philosophizing. In both cases, the attempt is made to remove the element of feeling or to regard it as a mere emotive accompaniment to a more rational form of behavior. In the present period, when science and its methodology have tended to dominate man's approach to his world, the absence of facticity in religion, its claim to knowledge of what transcends sense experience and is not scientifically verifiable, its consequent use of myth, symbol and poetic imagination, and its concern with feelingful awareness and the intuitive dimension of knowing—all these have supported attempts to reduce religion to the level of moral behavior. Likewise the attempt to defend religion in a rationalistic and intellectually skeptical environment has led to an over-intellectualizing.

Both these movements were evidenced in what we know as the Enlightenment. This period in the Eighteenth Century was marked by the tremendous success of the scientific approach to reality and the increasing emphasis on a rationalism which was intensely skeptical about the supernatural. The mathematical model of the universe, devised by Isaac Newton, was accepted as literal fact. A cosmos governed by scientific laws which could not be contravened by the natural processes ruled out miracle. Prayer could not be expected to influence a deity who, having created the world and its laws, now ruled in solitary splendor above its mechanism. Divine intervention could not be allowed. As Addison put it, in his hymn,

> Laws that never shall be broken
> For their guidance Thou hast made.

Newtonian science had produced a world which has been well described by Butterfield:

> God, the human soul and whole realm of spiritual things
> .... escaped imprisonment in the process of mechanization,
> and were superadded presences, flitting vaporously among
> the cog wheels, the pulleys, the steel castings of a relentless
> world machine. It was very difficult to show how these two
> planes of existence could ever have come to intersect, or at
> what point the mind or soul could ever join up with matter.
> (H. Butterfield, *The Origins of Modern Science*, London: G.
> Bell & Sons, Ltd., 1949, p. 110.)

Religion, insofar as it was accommodated to such a situation, assumed a deistic form. Any idea of miracle or divine revelation seemed to be excluded, for God was relegated to a lofty transcendence. Immediate awareness of the divine Presence could have no place in this scheme of things, and so other ways of understanding man's religiosity had to be sought. Out of such a situation came Immanuel Kant, with his emphasis on man's moral experience, and G. W. F. Hegel, with his view of the universe as a rational process.

Kant met the challenge of a Newtonian universe by postulating the scientific world as a phenomenal realm, largely the construct of the observing mind. Thus man's theoretical reason, operating upon the data provided by sense experience, could not reach beyond the phenomenal world which its sense experience and logical processes had largely created. Kant turned to man's moral experience. Although sense experience gave no valid knowledge of ultimate reality, he contended that the experience of moral oughtness, the compulsion of the categorical imperative, provided the necessary clue from which reason could legitimately arrive at a religious base for reality. Hence he could define religion as "the belief which sets what is essential in all adoration of God in human morality" (*Werke*, VII: 366), and, again, as "the recognition of all our duties as divine commands" (*Critique of Judgment*, II: 385). Kant thus rigorously excluded emotion and reduced religion to morality. Later, Matthew Arnold could add an emotional aura and describe religion as "morality touched with emotion."

In our time, the scientific atmosphere has made it still more difficult to justify religious experience, not because science is antithetical to religion, but because the increasing success of science has confirmed for many the belief that sense experience is the only viable way of knowing. In consequence, many have regarded any reality which transcends the natural process as illusory and religious language as nonsense, not conveying valid knowledge. In this atmosphere, R. B. Braithwaite, a philosopher of science, has taken refuge in the ethical dimension of religion. Dealing specifically with Christianity and clinging to his belief that observable experience is alone valid, he emphasizes the ethical aspect of religious behavior. He suggests that Christianity is characterized by a certain kind of moral behavior, describable as the way of love, agape, and illustrated by stories associated with the activity of Jesus Christ. He argues that "the primary use of religious assertions is to announce allegiance to a set of moral principles." Thus the thought of God fades into the background. So long as a man is committed to these moral principles, "he need not believe that the empirical propositions presented by the stories correspond to empirical fact" (*An Empiricist's View of the Nature of Religious Belief*, Cambridge: Cambridge University Press, 1955, pp. 17, 23). The reality of any personal disclosure of God and of any feelingful awareness of a divine Presence is bypassed, and belief content is reduced to a set of moral injunctions.

This reductionism at least retains the moral dimension of religious experience, but it ignores the feelingful awareness of a divine Presence which itself evokes the response of love and fear and which moves both the mind to intelligible understanding and the will to prayer and worship as well as moral behavior. Morality is generally regarded as an essential condition for communication with the deity, and religion has always been a conserver of moral values. We must not, however, believe that morality either creates the gods or is the central source for religious activity. Such a view of religion does not take account of all the data, even though it may try to explain them away.

Religion involves belief and endeavors in its theologies to give more rational and often abstract expression to what is pictured in its myths and symbols. In an age when rational concern with evidence occupies the center of the stage, it is easy to demand that religion be intellectually respectable. In doing so, it was easy for many of the deists of the 18th Century and their immediate successors to reduce religion to little better than a rational pursuit. The outstanding figure in this kind of thinking was G. W. F. Hegel. He believed that religion was a poetic and immature form of philosophizing, and that its mythical and symbolic forms attained their true meaning far better when expressed in the abstract structure of his own idealistic philosophy. Hegel assumed that One Mind constituted the sole reality of the universe and that its rational dialectic underlay the concrete forms assumed by individual persons and the natural and social structures in which they lived. Individual minds were the One Mind, the Absolute Spirit subjectivizing itself. They were adjectival existences of the One Mind and had no independent existence. Nature and society were objectified forms of the same Absolute, and, in the interrelationship of individual minds and these structures, the Absolute Mind was moving to self-realization. In such a highly abstract but logically developed world-view, religion could have no ultimate place except at the rational level. Its emotional aspect and its symbolic structures were incidental to the movement of the Absolute Spirit. What mattered was the rational dialectic to which religion contributed, and thus the basic truth of religion lay in the contribution it made to the self-knowledge of the Absolute Mind. We can therefore understand the definition of religion as "the knowledge possessed by the finite mind of its nature as absolute mind" or again as "the Divine Spirit's knowledge of itself through the mediation of the finite Spirit." For the individual mind was simply a manifestation of the Absolute Mind within the latter's historical pilgrimage. Religion must be stripped of its sensuous clothing, its pictorial and metaphorical forms, and interpreted in terms of pure thought.

In our contemporary scene, we are all familiar with the thought of Rudolf Bultmann. Concerned with the failure of religion, and specifically the Christian religion, to communicate with a secular order dominated by modern science, he sought to build a bridge across the gap between them. Recognizing that a science-oriented society finds it difficult to accept the mythical structures and miraculous events which are constituents of religious belief, he suggested a process of demythologizing. He would eliminate mythical thinking, which, as we shall see later, is essential in any understanding of a transcendent Presence. He would also do away with the ideas associated with the supernatural and a two-tiered universe, and replace the essential form of the religious message by a structure less repugnant to the modern mind. He finds the latter in the existential philosophy of Martin Heidegger. Thus, in a way similar to that of Hegel, he would strip away the outmoded and the sensuous and leave us with a religious credo expressed in the alien structures of a secular philosophy.

All this destroys the essence of religion, so we must turn from undue emphasis on the moral and the rational to consider a more balanced assessment of the data.

Feelingful Awareness and Patterned Presence

Kant and Hegel formed with Schleiermacher a triad of thinkers who have left a mark that still persists in our own time. It is to Schleiermacher that we must now turn our attention, for he emphasized the feeling content of the religious consciousness. Between them, this trio of thinkers covered every dimension of consciousness—conative, cognitive, affective—but there is little doubt that Schleiermacher got nearer to the essential aspect.

Schleiermacher, like the other two thinkers, was concerned especially with the Christian religion, but he and they were living in a time when the oriental world was opening up and knowledge of the other world-religions was in the ascendant. In consequence, Schleiermacher's analysis of the religious consciousness was given a much more universal background, and he was careful to examine the categories into which world religions may be classified.

In his own approach to the religious consciousness, two factors need to be noted. The first is his concern with the secular society of his time, already largely influenced by the scientific mentality. He desired to meet secular man at a point where he could make religious experience a viable possibility.

The second is his ontological methodology. Here he stands in the great Augustinian tradition and begins, not with the world, but with the immediate personal self-consciousness. Our consideration of this approach in the first chapter now needs to be amplified by a consideration of Augustine's thought, since this is very much in evidence in Schleiermacher's thinking. Augustine had taught that in being aware of ourselves, our transience and our finitude, we are also aware of the eternal and infinite Presence. Such self-awareness is internal and immediate. We exist, and we know that we exist. But such self-consciousness involves more than awareness of self. We know that we are not self-explanatory, and our self-awareness carries with it an immediate awareness of the Eternal Other. Augustine held that self-consciousness is God-consciousness. "In order to know God do not go outside yourself, return into yourself. The dwelling place of truth is in the inner man" (De Vera Religione, 39.72).

Schleiermacher took the same approach. He found the basis of religion in feeling. In his first book, Speeches on Religion to its Cultured Despisers, he describes religion as an immediate pious feeling and rejects both rationalism and morality as the keys to religious experience. This pious feeling is an immediate consciousness of the underlying infinite and eternal ground of all finite and temporal things. It is a direct feeling which transcends the subject/object dichotomy of intramundane knowledge and has immediate awareness of the Whole, the Eternal Being. We notice that, at this stage of his thinking,

Schleiermacher clings to two ideas—feeling, and an almost pantheistic view of deity which he describes variously as the Whole, the Universe, the World-Spirit, the Eternal Being. He uses feeling because he wants to show that religion has a distinctive approach to reality, distinguished from the approaches of science and morality. Yet he does not mean by feeling a pure emotional state with no objective reference. He is really speaking of a feelingful awareness. Indeed, he at first links up 'feeling' with 'intuition', but, in later editions of his book, he drops the second word and obviously includes its meaning in 'feeling'. He also calls it 'divination'. At this stage, Schleiermacher does not delineate feeling more carefully. Sometimes he generalizes pious feeling to include all healthy feelings. He is really, however, endeavoring to say that religious feeling is, at rock bottom, a feeling for the presence of the universe in the depths of one's own being. Pious feeling is something that all men may, or do experience of the surging life and pervasive power of the All, the Universe, operating upon them. True religion is the immediate awareness of God as he is found in ourselves and in the world.

The Augustinian tradition becomes more evident when Schleiermacher seeks to develop a theology. Now he identifies the religious feeling with immediate self-consciousness. Here his analysis is valuable, for he differentiates between man's immediate self-consciousness and his mediate self-consciousness. The latter arises from the nexus of relationships to the world and other persons into which man is 'thrown'. Man's selfhood is shaped by the intramundane and interpersonal relationships which this 'thrown-ness' makes possible. Mediate self-consciousness results from his reflection upon his selfhood which has been molded in this way. Through the mediation of his mundane and social environment he is aware of his individual personality.

But this is not the whole ego, for we are only fully self-conscious when a deeper relationship comes into play. This is the level of immediate self-consciousness. Here our self-awareness is not concerned with the objectively represented selfhood of reflective or mediate self-consciousness. Rather we know ourselves to be related to the Other who is the source both of our thrownness and also of all those other existents which have molded us into our selfhood. We are related to the Ground of our being.

Schleiermacher differentiates between the two forms of self-consciousness on the basis of freedom and dependence. In mediate self-awareness we know ourselves to be only relatively free, for we are also relatively dependent. In our thrownness, we have relative freedom to choose how the world of things and persons shall shape us and to shape that world to some degree. Yet we are also dependent upon the social, cultural and natural forces which that world brings to bear upon our lives. We cannot choose, however, where our 'thrownness' shall be in space or when our 'happenedness' shall occur in time. There is a radical dependence beneath our relative dependence and our relative freedom. Here we are not free. We cannot determine our time and place. We are not self-caused. Immediate self-consciousness makes us aware of this depth beneath, this Other who is the source and ground of our being, our 'happenedness'. There is no absolute freedom at this level of self-awareness but only absolute dependence. So Schleiermacher can define religion as a feeling of absolute dependence. He even styles it a pure feeling of absolute dependence, but the hidden agenda lies in the content of the 'feeling'. This is not pure unsullied emotion. It is a feelingful awareness of that Other on whom we absolutely depend. Feeling has cognitive content. Self-consciousness, at its deepest level, involves God-consciousness, and this God-consciousness is a feeling of absolute dependence.

Hegel criticized this kind of approach by suggesting that if the heart of religion were a feeling of dependence, then Schleiermacher's dog would be more pious than its master. It is, indeed, not a satisfactory definition of religion, but it does bring out the aspect of feeling in the religious consciousness. Schleiermacher was reacting, like many of his contemporaries, to the rationalism of the Enlightenment, by adopting a romanticist stance. His position needs to be considerably modified. He was far too immanentist in his viewpoint, for an over-emphasis on ontologism will always get near to pantheism. Indeed Spinoza's philosophy had a strong influence on Schleiermacher's thought, and he certainly tended to suggest a kinship between God and man which had a shallow view of sin and an inadequate understanding of the divine transcendence.

It is to Rudolf Otto that we must turn for a more adequate understanding of the feeling aspect of the religious consciousness. He undertook a careful phenomenological analysis of the religious response to reality, and, like Schleiermacher, sought to strip it of those elements which he attributed to the moral and rational dimensions of man's response to his environment. Once more we have the effort to identify something which is distinctively religious and cannot be explained as a form of or reduced to other types of experience.

Otto built on Schleiermacher's approach but held that the latter had not sufficiently differentiated the pious feeling. The difference from other feeling is not merely one of degree, as of absolute to relative dependence. The religious response has some measure of analogy to the feeling of dependence, but more is involved. Otto called it "creature feeling." This feeling has cognitive content but it cannot be verbally expressed. It must be directly experienced in order to be understood. It is "the note of self-abasement into nothingness before an overpowering, absolute might of some kind" (*The Idea of the Holy*, translated by J. W. Harvey, London: Oxford University Press, 1931, p. 10). Thus it is a feeling with objective reference.

Otto sought to define this objective reference, and employed the distinctive religious category of 'the Holy' to describe it. It is a valuation distinct from the valuations of the Good, the True, and the Beautiful. It is, however, a composite valuation and does involve elements of the other valuations. Thus the religious response has ethical and rational aspects, but they are secondary. The core of the Holy is a nonrational element which Otto conceptualized as the 'numinous'. This is the Holy stripped of all rational and ethical connotations, and it constitutes the unique religious concept or category for the evaluation of reality.

The numinous state of mind is the way Otto describes the religious consciousness. It is, for him, *sui generis*, and its object is a *mysterium* which transcends all conceptual expression. This mystery can be described as the "wholly other," an overpowering presence. It evokes a feeling of repulsion and attraction. It both daunts and allures, strikes fear and yet fascinates. It creates a feeling of utter self-abasement and nothingness, but it also evokes a feeling of love and attraction. This numinous feeling is one of awe before a towering majesty. Thus the object of the religious consciousness is described by Otto as the *mysterium tremendum et fascinans*, an overpowering Presence which daunts and yet attracts. This core of the religious object defies further expression. It is the Wholly Other, transcendent mystery. Religious awareness of this kind is a precondition for all developed religious responses. It belongs to the intuitive level of awareness and is a *sui generis* capacity for judgment and evaluation. Thereby religion has "its own independent roots in the hidden depths of the spirit itself" (ibid., p. 140). Indeed this category of the numinous is innate to the human consciousness and springs "from the deepest foundation of cognitive apprehension that the soul possesses" (ibid., p. 117).

Paul Tillich has gathered the emphasis of these thinkers into a form which meets the contemporary situation. Still standing in the Augustinian tradition with its ontological approach to reality, he concerns himself with the nature of man's self-awareness and in particular his awareness of his finitude. Man knows himself as a self having a world to which he belongs. He lives in a state of polarity in which self-consciousness and world-consciousness exist in tension. As a self-centered individual, he yet participates in his world, and his freedom is limited by his destiny as a part of that world. As he awakens to his own finitude, man also becomes aware of the unconditioned, of the infinite. Like Augustine and Schleiermacher before him, Tillich sees the awareness of God, the unconditioned, as the *prius* of man's awareness of his own finitude and of the subject/object dichotomy into which he is 'thrown'. This self-awareness is fraught with anxiety, for man knows himself to be living in the threat of non-being. Yet this anxious awareness of his finitude brings with it an immediate awareness of the Unconditioned. Thereby man is able to transcend his finitude to some degree and rise above his polarities. He knows himself both to be finite and yet to belong to the Ground of being, God. His anxiety about his own finitude is an ontological anxiety which also opens up an immediate awareness of God, the ground and power of our being. Tillich describes this as man's mystical *a priori*. It is the basis of all religious experience. The threat of losing meaning for his being, of encroaching non-being, creates a metaphysical 'shock' in which the depths of being are opened up. To be aware of one's finitude is also to be aware of God.

Tillich, however, regards feeling as only one aspect of this awareness, for will and cognition are involved. Schleiermacher recognized the cognitive aspect and Otto still more. Tillich, influenced by his own existentialist stance, emphasizes the will and the presence of commitment in the religious consciousness. He regards the primary immediate awareness of the Unconditioned as only the basis of religion. Religion truly arises when the ontological awareness attains content. What the awareness of the ground of being does is to raise the question of God. The awareness and question come together, and the question can only be answered by revelation.

Man looks for that which will enable him to transcend his polarities and rise above his finitude. Awareness of the presence of the unconditioned is not enough. The awareness must be filled with a content that gives meaning to his finite being and saves him in his totality. So man is driven by ultimate concern, a concern rooted in his primary awareness of God and his fundamental anxiety. In his finitude, with its threats of dissolution, he is concerned for that which gives his existence ultimate meaning, God. Religion is basically man's ultimate concern, that which he grasps cognitively as giving his life final meaning and that to which he is totally committed. God, as the religious object, helps man to rise above his polarities and find meaning in his finitude.

Thus Tillich brings out clearly the revelatory or objective aspect of the religious consciousness. We shall concern ourselves later with the nature of revelation. At this point, it is sufficient to note that the thinkers whom we have studied have emphasized a general and *a priori* awareness of the reality of God and have made this the basis of the religious approach to reality. The giving of rational content to the holy mystery is not discussed by Otto, and Schleiermacher, because of his tendency to pantheism, does not deal adequately with the issue of revelation. Tillich does, however, clearly stress the need for revelatory content in the general *a priori* awareness of the Unconditioned. If religion is ultimate concern, the different religions are to be distinguished by what their devotees regard as the nature of that concern, of God. Hence a final consideration of religion must take account of its revelatory content.

Now such revelation occurs at the level of our world-consciousness, even though it makes contact with us because of that *a priori* awareness of God in the deeps of our own self-consciousness. This is a reminder that, although we truly know ourselves from within and the world and other persons from without, we are aware of God both from within and from without. Otto's holy *mysterium* touches us through the depths of our environment as well as within where Schleiermacher and Tillich would place their bigger emphasis on *a priori* awareness of the divine. But it is from without, through the world and other persons, that revelation meets us. The God who comes to us in this way has a point of contact within our self-awareness. He does not come to us as a stranger, for already we are aware of him in the deeps of our personal being.

John Wisdom of Cambridge has employed a parable, also used by Antony Flew, to define religious claims to knowledge. Two explorers come upon a clearing in a jungle which appears to be a well tended garden. One of them contends that it must be tended by a gardener. The other denies it and regards it as an accident of nature. They decide to wait and watch, but no gardener appears. The suggestion that the gardener is invisible leads the skeptical explorer to suggest booby traps and electrified fences to keep the gardener out. Still there are no indications by shrieks or movements of the devices that anyone has tried to enter. The first explorer still persists in his assertion that there is an invisible gardener who has his own secret ways of looking after the garden that he loves. His skeptical companion despairs. Wisdom uses the parable to suggest that religion is concerned with discernment. The first explorer discerned a pattern in the garden which the skeptic did not see. Likewise religion grasps a pattern in the facts which may not be evident to others. The logic of experimental science cannot, as the parable suggests, deal with the depth claims of religion. It deals with the 'facts' of the world, but religion is concerned with a pattern in those facts which makes evident the reality of the transcendent Presence. Religion is a response to such a pattern, and religious language is concerned to direct attention to this pattern in facts, facts with which others are familiar. Thus Jesus of Nazareth becomes the Christ, because we discern in his life and death a pattern which is not evident to others. Revelation then becomes the disclosure of the divine Presence through certain patterning in nature and history. The pattern discloses the depth.

Imaginative Projection or Cosmic Disclosure

There have never been wanting those who dispute such a religious claim to divine disclosure. Religion may be a part of experience, but that does not mean that it has any claim to validity as a way of knowledge about reality.

Since Petronius argued that fear first created the gods, many have argued, in a similar way, that religion has no objective validity but is simply a manifestation of human subjectivity and imagination, even of psychological maladjustment. In more modern times, this kind of stance was adopted by Feuerbach. Influenced by Hegel, but rejecting

Hegel's idealism for a naturalistic approach to the universe, Feuerbach held that, apart from the reality of the natural order, all other experiences were the human mind positing imaginative objects for itself. Hegel's picture of the universe, in its totality, as moving to self-realization through the logical dialectic of subjective minds and objective structures of nature and society was thus stood on its head. The universal mind was replaced by the individual mind, and spiritual experiences became simply that mind objectivizing itself. Nature alone was excluded, for its actuality was necessary for the functioning of the human mind—nature needs man as man needs nature, and man can do nothing without nature. On the other hand, religion's claim to the actuality of God must be dismissed or explained away, for its object, God, is simply a projection of the human mind's inner dialectic.

Feuerbach had to explain the mechanism of such a projection. He found it in the opposition which nature presents to man's hopes and aspirations. Nature contradicts man's wishes and frustrates his dreams. He dreams of an ideal self, the attainment of which is opposed by his world. Man's inner knowledge of himself, purified and freed from the limits that beset him, is set up in an objective reality. The divine being is a projection of man's ideal self upon the backdrop of the universe. Hence, in religion, man is really revering and contemplating himself, idealized and objectified. Aware of his finitude, man seeks to be freed from it by his religion and creates a God in whose ideal image his wishes will be fulfilled. "God is my hidden, my assured existence, he is the subjectivity of subjects, the personality of persons" (*The Essence of Christianity*, translated by George Eliot, New York: Harper & Bros. 1957, p. 174).

Granted his naturalistic/humanistic stance, Feuerbach's position is logically valid. But it is so only within such a presupposition. His psychogenetic explanation of religion and God has been generally accepted by naturalistic thinkers ever since. Let it be said that he did endeavor to show that his position was a viable one, by explaining even the statements of the Christian faith on this basis. One fundamental error lay in his failure to understand the nature of religious language. Because it is full of anthropomorphisms, he assumed, in the light of his naturalistic humanism, that these must be taken literally, and not analogically. Hence religious statements about God were for him purely human, and the God to whom such human attributes are applied must be man himself. "If thy predicates are anthropomorphisms, the subject of them is an anthropomorphism" (*ibid.*, p. 17). The viable alternative to such a position, namely to accept the analogical nature of religious language, was barred to Feuerbach, as to all such subsequent thinkers," by his presupposition. He had no understanding of "felt analogies," such as those employed by Otto in his description of the numinous feeling.

We need to remember that Feuerbach, no more than any other thinker, can offer a rationale for his presupposition, since all our thinking takes place within the aegis of our absolute faith-hypothesis. We can however offer pointers to its veracity, and we can show how it illuminates all experience. This is what a naturalistic thinker tries to do, and often he makes the kind of reductionalism offered by Feuerbach quite attractive.

In more recent times, Freud has given a psychological turn to this position. His approach is so full of doctrinaire statements that his main support comes from his own interpretation of his case studies. His famous differentiation of the human psyche led to his view of religion as an illusion. He postulated an unconscious mind, consisting of a mass of interacting instinctual forces and impulses. This is the *id*, and its vital impulses were labelled the *libido*. Out of the unconscious id, the *ego* emerges and consciousness appears. The latter is actually directed by deep-seated motives, hidden in the unconscious, and our reason is really our conscious effort to justify our unconscious desires. We should not therefore expect Freud to offer a detailed argument for his position, even though he cannot avoid rational discourse. It is extraordinary how people will argue rationally to disprove the validity of reason and so belie their own argument! Not only does the ego modify the id, but in turn the ego is modified by the *superego*, the 'conscience'. The latter results from parents and other social groups imposing their will on the ego. Its beginnings lie back in the infantile state, when ultimately the father's will becomes dominant and the child takes over the father's standards as inner commands.

At this point religion begins. Freud sees it as a neurosis. When the father fails to provide security or becomes otherwise unavailable, the father-image is projected on the heavens as God. Religious belief is thus neurotic. The religious believer has never grown up. The inadequacy of a parent led him to project an adequate father-image on the heavens, and so he remains at the arrested stage of childhood. To escape the brutal realities and insecurities of life from which his father has failed to protect him, he creates a fantasy world which provides him with the security he lacks.

This position is immediately open to criticism. In the light of his stance, we should not expect Freud to argue logically. He presents his conclusions from clinical experience dogmatically and attacks his opponents on the ground that their attitude arises from unconscious inhibitions. But it is on the point of describing religion as a neurosis that the attack must be focused. There is no evidence to confirm this. It is by no means evident that all believers have a similar history of psychological development, as he would imply. Furthermore, there is no evidence that there are more neurotics among believers than unbelievers. Again, there is no evidence that normal people are generally atheistic and that the neurotic are religious. Indeed, religious people show often a stability and strength of character not at all associated with a neurotic state. Finally, neurotics tend to isolate themselves in their private fantasy world, whereas religion is generally a community affair.

It is, of course, true that mentally unbalanced persons hold religious beliefs and often tend to find a refuge in religion. But the fact that beliefs are sometimes held by neurotics in no way invalidates the beliefs. The truth or falsehood of a belief is in no way dependent on whether the believer is psychologically normal or unbalanced.

Freud's contemporary Jung, in his own way, also took up the projectionist position. He postulated a collective unconscious which underlay the personal consciousness and unconsciousness of each individual. In this collective unconscious were gathered the primordial archetypal images in which, during its early history, the human race had expressed its attitudes and reactions to the world. These archetypal images are condensed forms of man's early myth-making. They do not become effective until man faces a situation with which he is unable to deal. Then rational thought gives place to an upsurge of the unconscious which couches beneath. We take refuge in these mythological structures as they take life and assume religious forms. The familiar myths of the religions are thus traces of the primordial thought of the race. "The religious character of these ideas," writes Jung, "proceeds from the fact that they express the realities of the collective unconscious; hence they also have the power of releasing the latent energies of the unconscious"

(C. T. Jung, *Psychological Types*, translated by H. C. Baynes, New York: Harcourt, Brace & Co., 1938, p. 271).

Religious revelations can now be accounted for as the concretization of the archetypal images flowing up from the collective unconscious. God becomes a mythical deity, a psychological function of man. Jung quotes Scheffler's words:

> I know that without me
> God can no moment live.
> Were I to die, then He
> No longer would survive.
> I am God's child, His son,
> And He too is my child. . .

God becomes my projection, and the only ground of my being is the collective unconscious. At the best this is a kind of pantheism!

These psychological theories should remind us that psychological investigation neither confirms nor denies religious faith. It is one thing to investigate how religious faith arises, but this does not answer the question Why? Jung finds that religious faith helps to integrate the psyche, but this does not prove the reality or the unreality of God. His suggestion is that archetypal images in the collective unconscious rise into the consciousness, take religious form, and make such integration possible. But he has still to explain the presence of these images in the unconscious and why primitive man responded to his environment in this way. If he adopts the attitude that there is no objective reality which influences the human imagination in this way, it is because his tendency to a naturalistic stance would forbid it.

This criticism applies also to Freud and many subsequent depth-psychologists. Freud's analysis of the projection of the father-image depends for its validity upon his naturalistic presupposition. Yet the same process could be interpreted quite differently, if it be regarded as the way in which the deity evokes a response. To find the conditions under which religious belief arises is not the same as asserting that such conditions determine that belief. God may come to us through the father/son relationship, and this is the part-truth in Freud's highly naturalistic analysis. Truth depends upon rational demonstration, and not on psychological investigation!

The naturalist stands open to criticism on several counts. The fact that religious experience, in varied forms, is a universal phenomenon, should call in question any serious attempt to explain it away. For many people of many faiths, the hunger and thirst for God is very real. The strength of the urge to worship and to commit oneself to some cause, thereby finding personal fulfillment, is further testified to by the pseudo-ultimate concerns which men themselves create. Insofar as the naturalistic thinker is a scientist, he behaves as if the universe will respond to his rational probings. At this level he regards the universe as rational in structure. But, again, as a naturalist he accepts the fact that his natural hungers and desires can be met. Urges like sex and physical hunger have their objective counterparts. But if the universe makes sense and behaves in a rational way at these levels, why should it suddenly show a non-rational structure or be accused of irrationality when we reach the level of man's deeper and more spiritual desires. To rob man of a love for beauty, a yearning for the good, a burning desire for God, is to take away from life those deeper meanings which unify human existence. Presumably even the naturalist has a heuristic passion for truth, but a reasonable universe would hardly allow man to live so much of his life at the level of illusion.

The naturalist cannot see this because his reason only operates within the limits set by his absolute presupposition. Since we think as we do because we believe as we do, we cannot expect the naturalistic thinker to move outside his prior commitment. For, as has often been pointed out, the naturalist who believes in empirical evidence cannot prove his own absolute presupposition in that way. Furthermore, the naturalist appeals to reason to justify his claims, but ultimately any naturalistic approach dismisses reason as a reflection of, and as determined by, the natural process out of which the mind has emerged. Mind is a product of nature and controlled by naturalistic impulses, so what does any appeal to its reasoning really achieve? The truth is that such men can use reasoning to prove the universe irrational and, in so doing, deny their own premise.

One final point of criticism needs to be made. If we follow the theory of projection to its logical conclusion, then any mental and spiritual concepts whatsoever have no objective validity. Feuerbach, for instance, was logically bound to go this way since he concentrated on the self. He was only saved by irrationally postulating the objectivity of the natural order, and this naturalistic faith hypothesis provided his way out. To dismiss the idea of God as having no objective reality is surely irrational if we accept the objective validity of the concepts of science!

We do, however, need to note this dangerous challenge to any attempt to understand religion. Indeed, Karl Marx and his communist disciples have made it regnant over a large part of the earth's crust. They deny that religion has any validity save as an opiate of the people, a drug administered by the ruling caste, with the intent of keeping the proletariat contented with their impoverished lot. Religion offers 'a pie in the sky when you die' and thereby directs attention away from the intolerable situation of the present. It offers an escape into a hereafter where all will be well. Religion arises at life's limit-situations, like death and trouble, not in the midst of life. Ideas of God and heaven offer escape mechanisms which the capitalist gladly employs to keep the worker content. Now it has to be confessed that, to take Christianity as the outstanding Western religion, religion has often so emphasized the realm beyond death that it has ignored the social iniquities and the economic inequities of this world. Yet, at its best, a world-affirming religion has been a motivating force in transforming social structures and establishing some degree of social and economic justice. The history of the Christian Church demonstrates this. The same naturalistic presupposition underlies Marx's approach to reality as those of previous thinkers and the same criticisms apply.

We turn, therefore, to consider religion's claim to valid knowledge. We shall close this chapter by pointing to our criticism of Jung. We suggested that the archetypes of which he speaks resulted from the imaginative response of primitive man to an awareness of the divine presence. In other words, the myths which are the customary medium of cognitive expression in all religions are grounded in a cosmic disclosure.

There has always been a divine disclosure. Our studies in the earlier part of this chapter have supported this. Schleiermacher's God is the whence of his feeling of absolute dependence and, at this level, manifests little dynamic activity. Indeed Schleiermacher almost confines himself to such a general revelation, and even Jesus Christ is more on the human side as the perfect exemplar of the pious feeling. It is from his world-consciousness that man derives models which seem, at the moment, adequately to express his pious feeling, but there is no suggestion that this process is revelatory. Jesus Christ simply expresses the pious feeling most adequately. Otto's understanding of God as the holy mystery which both strikes fear and yet attracts suggests a dynamism that points to revelatory activity. Tillich accepts Otto's understanding of God as the holy and sees a form-denying as well as a form-creating aspect in deity, so that God is a living God, active, creative, revelatory. The two aspects of the Unconditioned are parallel to Otto's understanding of the Holy as both *tremendum* and *fascinans*.

This *a priori* awareness to which each of these thinkers points suggests little content. It involves a general revelation of the 'whence' of religious feeling, the mysterious presence of the Holy, the Unconditioned ground of being. Yet this is the basic immediate awareness from which all religions take their rise. It is a cosmic disclosure, a divine activity, of which all men are aware even when they deny it. As Tillich has pointed out, the question of God is only present because there is a prior awareness of God.

The presence of the mythical structures in the religious consciousness points back to those primordial religious experiences in which primitive man was conscious of the divine presence and imaginatively shaped his mythical forms. Mircea Eliade has made us much more aware of the profound significance of the myths present in the religious consciousness. For primitive man, these myths were not mere explanations of the mysterious occurrences in his world. As Ricoeur has pointed out, they had symbolic import. They offered an insight into divine activity and human response, into the relation of man to the holy mystery. Primitive explanation was undoubtedly present, but the myths also performed this symbolic role. They were molded on and pointed to the divine disclosure. Eliade points to the grounding of these myths in the cyclic view of the eternal return, so that the myths were the way in which primitive man was able to dwell under the aegis of the Sacred and to hold to "an ontology uncontaminated by time and becoming." This primitive type of 'ontologism' might suggest that, even at this primordial level, there were the beginnings of divine self-disclosure.

Such self-disclosure is more evident in the historical religions. Here specific religions claim their own particular revelations. These special revelations come through our world and are thus constituted by (to use Wisdom's suggestions) certain patterns in the observable structures of mundane existence. Other persons, nature, and/or historical events may manifest to the believing person a pattern which becomes a disclosure of the divine presence. That a person should recognize such presence is possible because, already in the deep places of the self-consciousness, there is an immediate awareness of God, even though it be tacit and unacknowledged. Such patterns of disclosure have the power of Being in them and evoke faith in the person who encounters them. Religion then comes to full flower, and feelingful awareness of the divine presence is filled with cognitive content. In the next chapter we must look at the nature of revelation and the cognitive structures which it awakens in the human consciousness.

We may, at this point, sum up our discussion of the nature of religion. We have sought to show that religion is no product of subjective imagining. There is a feelingful awareness of a given, a divine presence which comes both in the deeps of one's self-awareness and through the world of nature and persons. In the latter there is a disclosure of the mysterious and holy Other through a pattern which the believer discerns in his environment. This disclosure constitutes what he believes to be of ultimate and supreme value, that to which he is prepared to commit himself in his totality and which gives to his existence an integrating meaning. Thereby also the awareness of the divine is given communicable content. Apart from such special revelations which the great religions treasure as their ultimate concern, the divine awareness is that which can be felt "but it cannot be telt," as an old Scots woman said naively of her Christian experience. Mysticism stays at this level. Samuel Alexander describes religious experience as associated with worship, a sentiment through which "an object is made known or revealed to the person who has the feeling and he calls it God . . . Always, under whatever shape of sensible experience or fancy or reflection, there is the awareness of a mysterious something which enforces or pleads for recognition. And in that experience itself there is no question raised of whether the object experienced exists or not; it is for the worshipper as much a fact as a green leaf or the sun is for the dispassionate observer. The religious feeling and its object are given in one and the same experience" (article on "Theism and Pantheism" in the *Hibbert Journal*, Jan. 1927).

The Divine Disclosure
As Mediated Immediacy

3 Western philosophy began, as we have seen, with the Greeks. They are to be distinguished, as we have already noted, from the Hebrews by their emphasis on discussive logic and rational argument rather than on will and commitment. Indeed, their understanding of ultimate reality was quite distinct from that of the Hebrews. For the latter, ultimate reality was a personal deity who was characterized by dynamic will and purpose, an active, living God. For the Greeks, on the other hand, ultimate reality was static being, rational but not dynamic, to be arrived at through the reasoning processes and not through its own active disclosure.

Yet the Greeks were aware that this ultimate reality could be approached in two ways—within and without, through the inner self-awareness and through world-awareness. The Platonic tradition was a seedbed in some sense for both approaches. As it developed through Aristotle, however, it took the cosmological path. Its deity became the Unmoved Mover to be arrived at by deductive reason operating upon the knowledge of the world. The other development was through Neo-Platonism and took the ontological path. Such thinkers looked within rather than without. Self-consciousness took precedence over world-consciousness. It was 'within' that man was aware of Being, the ultimate ground of all beings. Awareness of himself was also awareness of his oneness with the ultimate. Along parallel lines the Stoics also had an ontological approach. Like the Neo-Platonists, the Stoics did not arrive at deity by logical inference from the observed character and behavior of external nature. Rather, they still, being Greek, believed in reason but they held that man carried innately in himself a knowledge of God. Every man had within a seed reason, a *logos spermatikos*, which was the immanent presence within of the world soul, the ultimate reality, God. They were ontologists in the full sense, holding that man had an inherent and immediate rational knowledge of God within, especially through his moral sense.

Largely because of the burgeoning knowledge of world religions and the increased understanding of their revelational claims, the emphasis has moved much more to revelation. Logical inference as a basis for natural knowledge of God and the idea of ultimate reality as static being have been replaced by the concern with knowledge through divine disclosure and the understanding of God as dynamic and active. Yet the Greek emphasis remains in the retention of the two ways in which knowledge of God may come—within and without. God meets men, both within the deep places of the soul and through the world of external experience.

So far we have emphasized both these ways in our analysis of the religious consciousness. Now we must examine such knowledge more carefully by concerning ourselves with the nature and the mode of the divine disclosures involved.

A Priori Awareness and General Revelation

We have seen two forms in which religious *a priori* awareness has been identified. Along the ontological path, followed by Augustine, Schleiermacher and Tillich, man is immediately aware of the Ground of being as he becomes aware of his own finitude. Self-awareness is, at the same time, God-awareness. I am immediately aware of the divine as I am aware of my self. This inner *a priori* awareness is matched in Otto's careful analysis by an *a priori* numinous feeling for the holy Mystery which transcends us and our world. The Mystery which both repels and allures is the transcendent depth in our environment. He meets us as the depth of our world as well as in the deep places of our innermost being. He presses in upon us as a Presence whom we cannot escape.

If these thinkers are to be accepted, we are beset on every hand by the divine presence. All of us have a tacit awareness of God even when we deny him. Indeed the divine is actively disclosing himself both within the deeps of our self-awareness and through the external world around us. Revelation is activity. God is the living God and, as such, he is everywhere confronting and imparting himself to his creatures. His pressure arouses our creaturely anxiety as we face the threat of finitude and nonbeing. Our tacit awareness of God sends us searching for the nature of that ultimate reality and for the concomitant meaning of our existence. The question of God besets us because we are already aware of him.

Yet that question cannot find an answer in our inner awareness. Here the infinite assumes no definable character. If we seek God only here we finish with mysticism. The inner awareness engenders a sense of immanence but little real awareness of transcendence. The sense of transcendence, as Otto makes clear, comes in the awareness of the *mysterium*, the Other which daunts and yet attracts, the awesome presence of the Holy. It is the disclosure through the world which begins to give structure to ultimate reality. The intuitive grasping of a *gestalt* (a pattern) in his world by the religious man arises because the Transcendent Presence is moving toward him in disclosure. The divine Mystery, the Holy, is actively evoking a response. In this *a priori* awareness of the Holy, man begins to sense the presence of grace and wrath in the depth of the universe.

Revelation as a Mediated Disclosure

We have noted that Schleiermacher, in a view too much flavored by his "*Kultar-Protestantismus*," suggested that the 'God-consciousness' within, the 'pious feeling' of absolute dependence, was filled with content by the 'world-consciousness' without. The influence of Spinoza and a consequent emphasis on divine immanence led him to regard the 'God-consciousness' as the real disclosure. Hence he ignored the issues of transcendence and of an understanding of revelation as mediated through the world. He held that the God-consciousness is universally present in all religions and receives specific embodiment in a particular religion because of the cultural milieu in which it finds expression. Specific religions have their characteristic theologies and ideas, but these are secondary. They arise out of reflection upon the 'pious feeling' or God-consciousness in the light of the culture in which they are formulated. Man's world-consciousness interacts with his God-consciousness to produce the variety of religions. This implies that every specific religion is a culture-religion and that what is significant in any one of them is its God-consciousness.

Schleiermacher does not, however, believe that the God-consciousness in any religion can be discovered by stripping off successive layers of cultural deposit, like skins off an onion, until only the core is left. Rather, the universal God-consciousness achieves a distinctive organic flowering in each religion. Each religion is an organic whole, not a mechanical structure of successive layers with the lowest layer that which the religion shares with all others. Thus knowledge of the God-consciousness flows from an intensive understanding of the particular religion in which one's own religious consciousness is expressed. Within that awareness, one must examine the relations of other religious embodiments to his own, seeking thereby to grasp the kernel of all religious experience, religion *per se*. As Niebuhr puts it: "however much a specific religious self-consciousness may approach the proportions of piety as it is recognizable everywhere, the identity of the former is always stamped with the particular character of the mediator of its appearance" (R. R. Niebuhr, *Schleiermacher on Christ and Religion*, New York: Charles Scribner's Sons, 1964, p. 230). But the revelation is that to which the basic pious feeling is a response, so that we have a general revelation but not any special revelations.

Paul Tillich has corrected Schleiermacher while retaining the latter's ontological approach. He has offered what is probably the ablest contemporary analysis of revelation. He emphasizes the ontological awareness of the Unconditioned and Infinite, the Holy, in the depths of man's self-awareness. But he joins to this the disclosure-situation in which the divine transcendence evokes a cognitive response through the varied media of man's world. It is the latter which gives religious faith its rich diversity of contents. The world-consciousness in this way mediates a divine revelation as the religious man is awakened to the presence of a pattern of depth in his world.

We may say that any dimension of our immediate experience of our world may, at the same time, be the medium of a divine disclosure. The beauty, austerity and awesomeness of nature may point beyond themselves to, and become media of, the divine presence. The movements of history may become disclosures of divine judgment and divine mercy. Individual persons, be they seers or sages, prophets or teachers, may become windows through whose words and teachings God gives to men a glimpse of himself. Here Plato, of whom Augustine said that he was a Christian before Christ came, stands among those like Isaiah who were media of a divine disclosure. The moral claim of others upon us may become a divine demand. The glimpse of truth may become a religious experience. The vision of beauty may become an experience of the beauty of holiness.

There is, indeed, no reality—thing, person, or group of persons—which may not be a medium of revelation. For all things are sustained by and have their being in God, and are thus open to his revealing activity. Tillich points out that "there is no difference between a stone and a person in their potentiality of becoming bearers of revelation" (P. Tillich, *Systematic Theology*, Vol. I, Chicago: University of Chicago Press, 1951, p. 118). He adds, however, that the things of nature do represent a lower aggregate of qualities that can thus point to the Ultimate Reality. Hence revelation through nature is more limited in respect to the truth and significance of what is thus mediated than is revelation through persons,

A revelation occurs when some thing, some person, some historical event takes on a miraculous quality and points beyond itself to the Transcendent Presence. Tillich suggests that it becomes 'transparent' to the divine mystery. It becomes a sign-event, manifesting to the discerning eye a pattern which is revelatory. The description 'transparent' is very appropriate, and we may develop this image by suggesting that the media vary in the degree and quality of transparency. Persons and groups of persons, including historical events, have a much higher capacity to serve as media of a divine disclosure than have entities belonging to the lower processes of nature.

The media of revelation do not possess revelatory power of themselves. They belong to the orders of nature and the realm of personal beings and are subject to the appropriate energies and urges. Thus a rainbow may be explained solely at the physical level as due to the refraction of light by its raindrops. It may be appreciated at the aesthetic level because of its array and pattern of colors. But only to the discerning eye of the biblical man of faith did it disclose the presence of a faithful and covenanting God. Or, again, let us consider the revelation which comes in history. When Assyria, motivated by imperialistic goals and the lust for power, attacked Judah, a purely historical analysis of the situation might be concerned with such motivating forces and with natural forces which might thwart Assyria's efforts, such as rats and plague. But the discerning eye of the prophet saw the pattern which betokened the divine activity in judgment and redemption. Thus a divine revelation does not take place *in* nature and *in* history but *through* nature and *through* history.

Tillich makes much of this in the case of historical revelation. He points out that what is important, when individuals or groups of persons become transparent to the divine presence, is not their historical importance or personal eminence, but the revelatory constellation into which they have entered under special conditions. The revelation through an historical occurrence cannot be foreseen or denied from the qualities of the persons or groups involved. It depends wholly upon the activity of the ultimate reality in which all live and move and have their being. Furthermore, a dimension of interpretation is required, as indeed such a dimension is a necessary ingredient in all historical knowledge. This dimension is provided especially when the particular historical occurrence includes the presence of a prophetic figure. He, together with the other historical forces, is gathered by the divine activity into a revelatory constellation. His discerning eye, divinely inspired, is made aware of the divine presence in the historical happening, and in the light of his revelatory interpretation a group may determine its historical destiny.

It is therefore not merely a peculiar immanent quality possessed by persons or natural forces which makes them mediators of revelation. Social preeminence and personal greatness do not make persons media, but rather the fact that the divine activity brings itself to a revelatory focus in them. A priest does not become a mediator of revelation because of his status and function, but under special conditions of divine activity. But then a prophet only manifests his peculiar qualities of insight when indwelt and inspired by the divine presence. A saint, too, is not revelatory simply because of his spiritual perfection, but only because he becomes transparent and enters, as a medium of revelation, into some divinely ordained situation. Prophets, priests, saints—all may become the bearers of revelation, when the divine Reality so chooses. They all have qualities which are appropriate to such 'transparency', but finally it is the divine activity which constitutes the revelation. The divine Presence is brought to focus in them in the light of the divine purpose.

The Cognitive Dimension of the Divine Disclosure—
Myth and Model

We have seen that the divine disclosure is God unveiling the mystery of his Presence. The Greek word for revelation—*apokaluptein*—means uncovering. It means the unveiling of a hidden meaning in something which may perhaps have been many times observed in a more superficial way. As W. M. Horton puts it: "In a crowded room full of veiled faces—and most faces wear a sort of veil, of impersonal unconcern—suddenly a veil is lifted, and another human face becomes full of meaning for me, perhaps in a way that will affect my whole destiny from then on" (*Christian Theology*, New York: Harper and Bros., 1955, p. 41). John Baillie has argued that the Greek word with its Latin and other linguistic equivalents is too exalted to be used naturally of merely imparting information, and that if it be so used, it is best appropriate to the unveiling of some mystery. It is not fundamentally concerned with the imparting of information but with self-disclosure and unveiling. John Baillie points out that we often use the word 'reveal' more loosely of conveying pieces of information, but that fundamentally we use it "of a man's revealing himself, that is, his character and mind and will, to his fellow" (*The Idea of Revelation*, New York: Columbia University Press, 1956, p. 27).

In biblical thought 'revelation' is always used in such an exalted sense. Thus Oepke can write that, in the New Testament, "revelation denotes, not the impartation of knowledge, but the actual unveiling of intrinsically hidden facts, or, theologically, the manifestation of transcendence within immanence" (*Theological Dictionary of the New Testament*, volume III, edited by G. Kittel, translated by G. Bromiley, Grand Rapids: Eerdmans, 1965, p. 591). In the Old Testament, likewise, the emphasis falls finally upon what God unveils of himself. It is a living encounter with God himself, and it is to be received only by those who wait upon him (Ps. 123). The content of such a revelation is not prudential advice or specific foretelling, but the living God. Herrmann has declared of the biblical usage that "all revelation is the self-revelation of God" (W. Herrmann, *Offenbarung und Wunder*, Glessen, 1908, p. 10, cited in J. Baillie, *The Idea*, p. 34).

If we follow this understanding and take the biblical understanding as the norm, the divine revelation is God's self-disclosure, not a set of propositions about God. Credal statements and theological propositions are not the initial disclosure. They are human attempts to formulate in communicable form the reality of that divine Presence which has been disclosed. In recent years, it has been increasingly emphasized that revelation is not the imparting of a set of religious truths to men by God. William Temple has written: "There is no such thing as revealed truth. There are truths of revelation; but they are not themselves directly revealed" (*Nature, Man and God*, London: Macmillan & Co., Ltd., 1924, p. 316). We do not receive divinely guaranteed truths through revelation. Thus, again in Temple's words, "what is offered to man's apprehension in any specific revelation is not truth concerning God but the living God Himself" (ibid., p. 322). Now it is true that such an understanding of revelation is brought to a focus in the Judaeo-Christian religions and that Temple takes these as his specific template. We have suggested the same, and shall attempt to support this position shortly. All this means that revelation is fundamentally a self-disclosure, an active impartation of the divine Presence. Further, our discussion suggests that such revelation and self-disclosure is meeting men everywhere and is brought to a focus in certain persons and historical events where it is given clearer content.

Now to use the phrase 'self-disclosure' is to suggest that the ultimate reality is at least personal. The Transcendent Presence comes to us through the media of the world and human persons, creating within them patterns which point like vectors to and disclose the depth beneath. Thereby the veil which hides much of the divine mystery is lifted. It is significant that when the Transcendent thus approaches man through the empirically sensed media of the disclosure situation, the encounter takes a form akin to our own personal being. Even when men identify the media of revelation with the deity and fall into idolatry, they ascribe personal qualities to even natural objects. Furthermore, primitive man's response to the divine Presence is made explicit in myths and symbols which employ personal structures and follow personal patterns. In his worship, the core of religious experience, man is responding to a personal mystery.

The truth would seem to be that man can never truly worship or offer his reverence to what is less than himself. When we find a genuine experience of the Holy, with all that such an immediate appraisal involves, our emotions, when truly self-critical, will not permit us to stand in awe of that which is not at least personal. The

Holy may be supra-personal, but such a presence can never be sub-personal if it evokes our rational response of worship and commitment. It is significant that even the religions like Hinduism which take the mystic path and claim to transcend the personal fall into sects which rehabilitate the personal or take paths in the Bhagavadgita and the system of Ramanuja which represent the deity in personal terms, even though the tendency always remains to deny the world and to discount the significance of finite personal being. But where the world is affirmed and a realistic approach is central, as in the great historical religions of Judaism, Christianity, and Islam, the vision of the Transcendent is always portrayed in personal form.

In these religions, in actual fact, Otto's numinous feeling is filled out with deeper significance in the historical disclosures of the divine Presence. Men become aware of God as absolute demand and final succor, to borrow H. H. Farmer's description. Here is something akin to our experience of other finite persons. Our experience of other persons involves an encounter of active agents, of wills that both resist and cooperate. The other's will sets limits to our own activity. At such limits resistance and demand meet us, but there may also be cooperation and commitment. The other can frustrate our purposes and make counter demands, or he can cooperate with us and further their fulfilment. Demand and succor are both present. When we broaden the base of Otto's numinous feeling to embrace the moral and rational dimensions in religious experience, we find ourselves using personal terms to speak of God. He is beyond our human polarities. He is the final and absolute limit to all our relative freedom and dependence. Yet he comes to us in an absolute and final way as demand and succor, as judgment and grace, as claim and love. God is felt as dynamic personal will. Man realizes a divine givenness, akin to his own personal being, yet providing his final limiting horizon.

Already it is clear that man can only portray the utter uniqueness of divine disclosure in forms and experiences taken from the intramundane and interpersonal level of relations. Since the ultimate reality is the transcendent Mystery, the Holy Other, the ground of all that is, we cannot portray or communicate its otherness and uniqueness except in such a way. Even then we can only point. The natural language of religion, just because it does deal with the unique, with ultimate transcendent mystery, the 'particular of all particulars', is the language of simile and metaphor, of poetry, of allusive reference and pointing, of analogy and model.

Here we may begin with man's mythical consciousness for we are very aware today of how significant this is in man's attempt to express and communicate the divine disclosure which has come to him. We have already dismissed Jung's attempt to reduce the objective reality of God to a projection of the archetypal images which, for him, reside in a collective unconscious of the human race. Much of his thinking is highly hypothetical, but he has done us a service by reminding us of the significant mythical structures and images which are buried deep in the racial memory. The unacceptable nature of his theory must not blind us to his concern with man's mythical consciousness. Thanks to the work of philosophers like Ernst Cassirer and W. M. Urban, the last decades have seen an increasing emphasis on the place of myth and symbol in the religious consciousness. As scholars have explored the religious behavior of primitive man, they have made it very evident that his myths expressed a genuine response to spiritual reality and that this response was acted out in his religious ritual, often in dancing. Thus religious myths were acted out as well as orally communicated. Nor are the more developed religions free of this emphasis. Rather myth and symbol are basic in the cognitive aspect of the religious consciousness, and basic to the understanding and communication of that divine disclosure which any specific religion regards as central and authoritative.

We have already emphasized this in our critique of Jung's theory. The religious myths are not mere primitive explanations of phenomena and of life's mysteries, but rather bound up with the divine self-disclosure. It is, however, unfortunate that ever since the time of Voltaire, the former view has persisted. Myths have been identified with outmoded and prescientific explanations, and therefore as equivalent to fables, legends, and fairy stories. They have no ground in reality but are regarded as fiction, as incredible and untrue, as the outmoded products and deposits of man's primitive imagination and thinking. In actual fact just the opposite is the case: religious myth is profoundly true. It contains insights and expresses depths in a divine disclosure which the abstract language and prosaic utterance of modern man, with his arrogant claims to maturity, can never express. Deep in all religious experience, the human imagination has been so captured by the Transcendent Presence that it shapes the myths and symbols, poetic analogies and models to communicate the insights which are given in a particular disclosure. For this is what myths and symbols are—analogies, models, images. They belong to the realm of poetry, of imaginative creativity. They point to the depths of reality and, like poetry, evoke insight into those depths. Indeed the human imagination is working under the pressure and influence of the divine disclosure in forming them, even though it may take a long period of maturation for them to take their final form in the religious groups which regard them as significant ways of expressing the faith.

The French scholar, Ricoeur, has undertaken an exhaustive phenomenological examination of myth and symbol. He contends that the level of myth is still a primary one for insight into the spiritual realm. There are dimensions of religious experience which can only be adequately expressed in mythical terms (P. Ricoeur, *The Symbolism of Evil*, New York: Harper & Row, 1967, pp. 161ff. and 306ff.). Once we translate such insights into abstract philosophical concepts, as does Bultmann with his use of Heidegger's existentialism, or into allegorical interpretation, we miss the depths of meaning which the religious symbolism contains. In man's symbolic understanding of the deity and of himself in relation to deity, there is always a depth which expresses the disclosure of the transcendent Presence and which discursive logic and abstract thought are less adequate to express. For Ricoeur myth and symbol constitute a unique and authentic mode of communication.

Mircea Eliade has argued that, through his myths, primitive man escaped from the profane and found the true meaning of life in the sacred. The myths conveyed the reality of the sacred. Usually grounded in a cyclic view of time, because of man's nearness to the natural order and dependence upon it for survival, such myths at appropriate times enabled man to return to the sacred for inspiration and power. Eliade would thus contend that myths are expressions of the divine Presence. Deeds and rituals performed in conformance to such myths opened up communion with that Presence and made available the power of the sacred. Religious myths and symbols provided the framework for uncovering ultimate reality and enabling man to live in the sacred. At appropriate holy times and in appropriate holy places, such a framework became operative in man's consciousness and the depth of reality was opened up to him.

Profane time, as Eliade points out, is linear. As man dwelt increasingly in the profane and a sense of history developed, the desire to escape into the sacred began to drop in the background. The myths, tied up with cyclic time, were not so easily operative. Secular man could control and manipulate his world and felt less need for dwelling in the sacred space. Indeed the sacred could not be controlled like the secular. The myths and rituals which enshrined the disclosure of the divine reality required conformance to the demands of the sacred. Man must mold himself to the shape of the divine disclosure. So secular man became content with his linear time. He could not return to cyclic time and re-enter sacred space through its myths.

Just here, as Eliade sees it, a new religious structure became available. In the Judaeo-Christian religions—Judaism, Christianity, Islam—history is taken seriously, and linear time is accepted. The cyclic time of the primordial mythical consciousness has been transformed into the time of profane man, but the mythical consciousness remains. It has been historicized. The Christian mythos and its accompanying ritual are bound up, for example, with history and center in authentic history, especially the Christ-event. Sacred space, the Transcendent Presence, is thus opened up to secular man because it meets him where he is, in the linear flow of secular time. The Christian myth gives such time a beginning in creation, a center in the Christ-event, and an end in the final consummation.

The real issue at the level of the mythical consciousness is the hermeneutical one. Evidently we must not regard the central significance of myth as primitive and immature explanation, even though the aspect of explanation is there. Much more important is the symbolic role of myth in disclosing the relation of man and his world to the Transcendent. Ricoeur holds that there is a primitive *naiveté*, and that this needs to be removed. But myth offers an insight into divine activity and human response which goes far deeper than any primitive explanation. Reinhold Niebuhr, before Ricoeur's work, had pointed to the permanent and transient aspects of myth. The transient is bound up with primitive world-structure *(Weltbilt)* and such explanation must be discarded. It is bound up with an outmoded culture. The permanent is the continuing revelation of the

Transcendent, and its symbolism must be retained. What we need, according to Ricoeur, is a mature *naiveté*, a hermeneutic of the symbolic role which the myths can still perform. As Jasper has put it, we have to read the ciphers which Transcendence offers to us.

This discussion of myths and their symbolic function brings us to a full consideration of the cognitive aspect of the divine disclosure. The experience of such a disclosure has to be formulated mentally and communicated. Since God is unique and transcends all our conceptualizing, we can only express the personal self-disclosure in analogical form. Intramundane activities and feelings which come nearest to what we experience at the religious level become the material for our analogies. In particular, interpersonal relations are highly significant, for if God be at least personal, we may find models for understanding and communicating the disclosure in such relationships. This is certainly true of the religions embraced within the Judaeo-Christian grouping.

The use of the word 'model' here is valuable because it is a description frequently used in the natural sciences to describe efforts to understand some phenomenon. Here analogies or models are taken from areas of investigation with which the scientist is familiar and made the basis for seeking to understand some observed phenomenon for which no intelligible explanation seems available. Thus the planetary structure of the solar system and the wave structure of light have been employed to explore and explain the structure of the atom and the behavior and nature of subatomic particles. Nobody takes such models literally but they are regarded as useful models which point the way to a deeper understanding and better control of some observed phenomenon. Indeed, the models are modified and even discarded as understanding progresses. At best, such models are analogies with sufficient similarity to what is observed to provide clues for a better understanding. Thus the electron is pictured by two models—particles and waves. Sometimes its behavior is better explained by the corpuscular model. At other times the wave model is significant.

In the same way, models help us to understand the divine self-disclosure and make it intelligible to others, as well as offering a rational base for our own thinking and a meaningful base for our practical living. Thus the divine disclosure itself has an analogy in our relationship to other persons. As I. T. Ramsey points out, there are moments in our relationship to others when a disclosure-situation arises and the other reveals himself or herself to us in word or deed. Suddenly the bodily behavior and stance, the tone of voice and the expression of face, the words employed, become revelatory. They become transparent to a personal depth, and we feel that we understand better the real person. The inner ego has been, for a moment, unveiled. We talk often about "falling in love" or about "understanding someone better." When we say this, we are referring to disclosure situations. Hence it is not surprising that the personal model is so central in our understanding of the divine reality. God may, in his transcendence, be far more than personal, but he is at least personal.

A personal model is an analogy. It must not be taken literally, but it has sufficient likeness for it to give a clue for the understanding of the divine self-disclosure. Thus we have analogies based on personal status—father, son, king, lord; we have analogies based on personal power—mighty one; we have analogies based on human psychological functions—will, mind, and so forth; we have 'felt analogies' based on human feelings and reactions—love, wrath, patience, long-suffering, mercy; we have analogies based on qualities of human character—faithfulness, goodness, righteousness, integrity. And so we could continue, for all the best characteristics, qualities and aspects of human nature are applied analogically to God in the religions of mankind.

Often, indeed frequently, naturalistic thinkers have accused religious people of talking nonsense. They can make this accusation since they deny the reality of a spiritual order and of a two-tier universe. Living in their kind of world, they deny any transcendence and therefore regard religious language univocally. And if it is taken literally, religious language does mean nothing. At this level, since its immediate referent is the human person, its anthropomorphisms do not make sense. If, on the other hand, it is understood analogically and symbolically, it can be very meaningful as pointing to the Transcendent Presence. Since the latter is beyond sense experience, a literal and univocal understanding of religious language would be impossible. But the words are employed symbolically. They describe models, felt and other analogies, by which the religious person is endeavoring to express an apprehension of the awesome, all-embracing, ultimate Reality, who comes to us as a personal Presence.

I. T. Ramsey suggests that religious language is always odd language. To indicate that it points beyond any relation it may have to intramundane experience, it adds qualifiers to the models which it employs. These qualifiers prohibit it from being taken literally. Because God is known to us as infinite dynamic personhood, he is love, wisdom, power, will, and other qualities, *et al*, yet more. All that we find in man at the best we find infinitely more in his self-disclosure and in our growing experience of his presence. So we add adjectival qualifiers to express more clearly how our models must be understood. He is love, but he is *almighty* love. He is wisdom, but he is *infinite* wisdom. He is creator too, but for the great historical religions he is *absolute* creator. He creates out of nothing, *ex nihilo*. He is not limited by pre-existent and independent stuff in his creating, just as in his love he is all-powerful. God exercises moral claim, but his is *absolute* demand. So, too, we may speak of him as *first* cause or uncaused cause, borrowing again from the idea of cause in our intramundane experience. He is powerful, but he is *all*-powerful, *omni*potent. He is a real presence, but he is present everywhere; he is *omnipresent*. In using these qualifiers the religious man is pointing, but he is also seeking to make his faith intelligible. He is trying to speak of the unique, and singular, while employing universal concepts which apply to the many in his world. Those concepts provide his models, and the models point to the singular. The facticity of his statements about God must be in the self-disclosure itself. All he can hope is that, by using sufficient models with the appropriate qualifiers, he can provide enough clues for another to enter into the same disclosure situation. The other person cannot understand until he has been where the religious man has been. As the models we develop cluster around the central symbol 'God', they expand and become clues which make a disclosure possible.

All this should not surprise us, for even at the personal level it is difficult to speak of any individual person without using paradoxical descriptions. Attempts to describe the personal qualities of someone fall into some degree of logical disorder. Every person is a 'singular one', as Kierkegaard would have said. And the singular cannot be expressed in universal or conceptual form without logical and rational order being broken. The only way to avoid this is to point and use the proper name of the person concerned. But we do need to express some of what we are aware in their personal self-disclosure to us. The difficulty of this is seen in the case of people who fall in love. They have difficulty in describing the unique quality which has attracted them to the other person. Personal appearances have characteristics that are shared with others—brown eyes, golden hair, etc. Finally, they have to lean back on the unique John Doeness or Sara Doeness of the object of affection. Langmead Cosserley has made the point that universal and general concepts can often be applied paradoxically as we seek to describe the subjectivity, the inner I-ness, of another person. He notes the use of paradox in the classic description of James I as "the wisest fool in Christendom." Only a person in his singularity can be wise and a fool at the same time! In this sense we might describe paradox as the holding of seemingly contradictory concepts in polaric relationship. In human relationships of love and mutual understanding, our expressions of our immediate awareness of the other can never adequately express what we feel. The synthetic reason grasps a personal whole which the analytical reason can express only in paradoxical form. There is a residual mystery in the inner core of personality which the analytical reason and its logical processes cannot penetrate; the knowledge of love grasps more than can be expressed. But if this holds of the mystery of finite personhood, how much more must it hold of the Singular of all singulars, the unique and ultimate mystery of love and will and reason! The symbolic must always remain at the center of religious thinking, illuminating out of the depths of its models and analogies our understanding of God and of man, in all facets of human experience.

Religious Diversity and Revelation Claims

We have seen that all men are aware of God even when they deny him. As Anselm put it, you cannot deny that of which you are not aware. Or, in the words of his great mentor, Augustine, men are made for God as the sparks fly upwards. This does not mean they worship the divine reality. Rather they mishandle their freedom and turn their back on God. In their alienation, they may mishandle the genuine divine disclosure in two ways. The first way is to create a pseudo-religion of their own from which the divine disclosure is absent. The second way is to distort the divine disclosure so that the content of the religious faith is inadequate and ineffective.

The first way of pseudo-religion is man's search for an authentic existence which ignores the divine Presence. He seeks authenticity autonomously, by centering his life in himself, or heteronomously, by losing himself in the crowd or identifying himself with the naturalistic urges of his animal background. In this way, man tends to form false ultimate concerns (to use Tillich's phrase), to find unifying meaning in the pursuit of political ambitions, social status, economic success, or in subjection to a collectivist state, or in allowing himself to be controlled by his animal desires and biological hungers. Life is full of such false ultimate concerns. They become surrogates for the living God and are the false gods of a secular or naturalistic society. They require subjugation to their particular rules and laws in order to attain the promised fulfillment. But, in various ways, that promised fulfillment turns out to be an empty thing. Such false gods prove their falsity by their failure to unify life at the practical level. Plays like "Cat on a Hot Tin Roof" remind us of the way in which the attainment of wealth brings, not fulfillment, but frustration and emptiness. Our generation is beginning to discover, too, that practical naturalism can make life turn to ashes and leave men in despair. The escape mechanisms of our day, including drugs and sex, are leaving life sorely strewn with wreckage. Man's incurable religiosity even turns him now to demon worship, with its accompanying sex orgies and its psychic abnormalities. Here we see what happens when man seeks to create his own gods.

The second way of distortion of the divine disclosure arises when men are confronted by a divine disclosure but, in their alienation and blindness, identify the ultimate Presence with the medium through which the divine disclosure comes to them. Hence the sun and the heavenly bodies, mountains and trees, sticks and stones become objects of worship. Man worships the forces of nature, creates fertility cults, worships the forces of procreation, fabricates idols, even elevates his kings and priests to a divine status. This can happen with Christian preachers!

Yet here genuine religion, in its central aspect of worship, is present. It is significant that, even when man does worship natural forces or objects, he attributes personal qualities to them. In his imagination, he tells myths about them which lift them to the level of personal activities and responses. From animism through polytheism to the many forms of monotheism, man has felt the presence of the personal. His religious imagination has produced myths and symbols which suggest that he is responding, however blindly, to a personal Presence. Even when he seems to be worshipping at the level of nature, nature and its forces are personified. Where man's pseudo-ultimate concerns bring him to the point of worship as, for example, in the case of the collectivist state and totalitarian ideologies, the religious urge is brought to a focus in some personal figure like a dictator or a dead hero whose tomb perpetuates a national myth, a Hitler or a Lenin. And if a man's ultimate concern is linked up with his own ambitions, do we not speak of self-worship?

Yet when we dismissed such false deities and idolatrous distortions, we still have to face the fact that, where religion is genuine and authentic, there is a wide variety in its understanding of the nature and purpose of ultimate reality, of God. Religions are by no means agreed as to the models that they employ and the understanding of deity which they cherish.

The great religions have, since the time of Schleiermacher, been classified in two major groups—the mystical or ontological type and the moral or teleogical type. They would cover respectively the religions of the Orient—Hinduism, Buddhism, Taoism, and the religions which originated in the Near East—Judaism, Christianity and Islam. The latter group are also styled historical or prophetic, since they are bound up with historical disclosures associated with prophetic figures.

Tillich justifiably describes the mystical religions as ontological. They are fundamentally bound up with the presence of the Deity in the depths of the self-conscious mind and tend to turn within. They therefore stress the divine immanence and are frequently pantheistic. God is met within man's self-awareness and not through the world. Indeed, such religions are generally world-denying and would not regard the world as a medium of divine disclosure. Hinduism is a prime example of this. It is best understood in its great Upanishad period. Here we have a mystical concern with the identity of the human spirit, the Atman, with the ultimate spiritual reality, the Brahman. Here the divine Presence transcends good and evil and might be described as supra-personal. Yet it is significant that the Hindu sects like the Vishnuites and the religious concern associated with the Bhagavadgita and the system of Ramanuja envisage the deity in personal terms and emphasize the divine grace and compassion. Furthermore, the acosmic and world-denying attitude of the Upanishads is modified by some measure of accommodation to the reality of this world. Generally, however, the world and human history are of small significance, and the fundamental insight is in what we have called the *a priori* awareness present in the personal self-consciousness.

Buddhism, in its Hinayana or Theravada form, is little more than a psychological system for killing desire, yet it is drastically acosmic and world-denying, despite its ethical precepts. The issues of whether it is atheistic and what is meant by Nirvana need not concern us, except to indicate that any religious claims it has would point to mystical absorption in deity at the best. Yet again, the Mahayana form of Buddhism falls back upon a personal understanding of deity and gives personal survival a significant place. Generally we may say that the divine Presence is envisaged at least in personal form but that there is a tendency to discount the significance of finite personal being. The philosophical systems tend to oscillate between acosmic pantheism and panentheism.

The historical, moral, teleogical group of religions builds on historical disclosures in which prophetic figures are central. Here God is presented in personal terms and the human person is given full significance with freedom and capacity for moral decision. We move from a world-denying to a world-affirming stance. This world of immediate experience and its historical movement become the arena for the fulfillment of the divine purpose. Here the divine will deals in judgment and in mercy with human freedom and personal decision. Finally, absorption mysticism gives place to communion mysticism. Men have fellowship with the deity to a point where the characteristics of mysticism became evident. However, where the basic divine disclosures are adhered to, the believer does not lose his personal identity. God is personal, and finite personal being is regarded as of supreme worth. We notice, furthermore, that mystical contemplation recedes into the background before an emphasis on moral action in the social and natural arena. Men's faith is expressed by their action in the world. Alienation and estrangement are overcome, not by mystical absorption but by moral obedience and divine grace. The philosophical systems in this group vary from theism to deism with the main form being ethical theism.

The Issue of Finality

The issue of finality now lifts its head. Is the diversity such that no religion stands out as a norm against which the others may be measured? Are we dealing with a multiplicity and can we expect no final manifestation of the religious consciousness?

Ever since the time of Schleiermacher, the impact of the contemporary culture upon a flowering of the religious consciousness has been recognized. Since, in our own discussion, it is this contemporary scene which provides the medium for the divine disclosure claimed by any religion, it is evident that there is a profound interaction between any religion and its cultural milieu. But, of course, such interaction is not a one-way street, for a religious flowering can create a new culture or recreate the culture in which it comes to birth.

A leading exponent of the emphasis of multiplicity has been Troeltsch, whose work is still influential and is actually enjoying a revival of interest. Professor at the University of Berlin, he was influenced by his great predecessors, Schleiermacher and Hegel. Thanks to their thought, his emphasis was immanentist. He was much concerned with the nature of history and emphasized the relativity of all historical phenomena. All the values of history are relative, and there can be no absolute in history. This did not, however, mean that Troeltsch denied the reality of divine revelation. Rather he believed that history is pervaded by reason and directed by infinite Spirit. This immanent reason, God, is the source of all historical appearance, and all history is a revelation of its life. Any idea of theistic transcendence and of the supernatural was thus banished. All that Troeltsch would admit was that God was a suprasensible reality standing beyond historical appearances and in this sense transcendent.

Since history is a rational unfolding of the Spirit, there is no special self-disclosure of God. Rather revelation is practically synonymous with discovery, since religion arises through the work of the immanent Spirit within the human consciousness. It is a feeling of "the presence of the whole within ourselves" (cited in my *Positive Religion in a Revolutionary Time*, p. 132). Thus Troeltsch was prepared to accept a religious *a priori* structure in the human consciousness. Religion is a special category associated with the apprehended presence of the Superhuman and Infinite in the human soul. This religious *a priori* makes man inherently religious and provides the point of contact which makes possible the reception of the divine revelation. We must remember, however, what Troeltsch means by the latter. Revelation is primarily the all-pervading presence of the Suprasensible Reality grasped intuitively by the religious *a priori*.

Since the divine presence is everywhere the same, we can expect no finality in man's religious development. All religions serve their purpose. Each plays its part in the elevation of humanity to God within the process of human history. The divine ground of the whole process sets the goal for historical development, so the coming of any religion is no contingent occurrence. Within all this relativity, Troeltsch was, in his earlier thought, prepared to grant some measure of finality to Christianity. He saw it as the historical point of convergence of two streams of religious movement—religions of law, exemplified in Judaism and Islam, and religions of redemption, exemplified in Hinduism and Buddhism. Hence Christianity had the highest claim to universality of all religions. Later, however, under the pressure of his relativism, Troeltsch moved away from this position. Increasingly he bound religion and culture together. Each religion must be viewed as the integrating center of a cultural phenomenon. As such, Christianity is distinctive as the religious center of Western culture. We must, according to Troeltsch, see history as a continuing manifestation of ever new and peculiar individualizations of the divine life, and we must certainly not look for unity or universality among them. Christianity is the only valid religion for us in the West, since it has grown up with us. It is the way in which we receive and react to the divine revelation, allowing for the kind of beings that Westerners are. Therefore, for us, but only for us, it is final and unconditional. Other groups, in different cultural situations, will experience the presence of the divine life in different ways.

Troeltsch was prophetic in the sense that he recognized the impact of science and the dawn of a secular age. He could not find a place for the supernatural and for theistic transcendence. He would not, however, sell out to naturalism, for he believed that history had a place for individuality and an element of freedom. The forces that made history, however, must be within history itself. God was suprasensible but immanent, pervading the whole process and directing it to its future goal. The latter was a religious one—the ultimate union of the finite spirit with the Divine Spirit that indwells it. The only absolute in history is the divine life within it, and all cultural flowerings with their religious centers are relative. Granted his presupposition, we can understand why Troeltsch was a relativist. If there be no transcendence, revelation does become akin to discovery, and the only answer to secularity is to treat all history as a movement of an immanent divine life. He did, at least, recognize that every religion has a measure of revelation and was not just man-made.

Troeltsch's attempt to give some degree of finality to Christianity by regarding it as the convergence of two religious streams does provide a clue to the issue which we are discussing. This was taken up by H. H. Farmer as a basis for establishing the finality. Farmer begins where our own emphasis falls, on the personal nature of the divine self-disclosure. He believes that religion is always a personal relationship to a personal God and that the core of every revelation is its dimension of personal response to a divine disclosure. Religion arises where the disclosure of ultimate reality is personal. Christianity must be placed alongside all the other religions on this basis, for it shares with them this common essence. Here Farmer faces the issue of relativism. Is Christianity one of a class or has it a uniqueness which positions it in a place apart?

In his consideration of this issue he finds help in the thought of R. G. Collingwood. The latter has pointed out that classification at the level of moral and spiritual matters differs from that at the level of the natural sciences. In the latter, the boundaries between the classes are clear and distinct. The members of a class may differ in degree but never in kind. Classes are mutually exclusive. When, however, we turn to the "sciences of the spirit," the classes overlap. Degrees of difference within a class may be so great that they merge into a difference of kind. Thus traditional logic does not apply at this level of experience. In the area of moral values and spiritual phenomena, "difference of degree, when it reaches a certain point, may become a difference of kind without ceasing to be a difference of degree" (H. H. Farmer, *Revelation and Religion*, New York: Harper & Bros., 1954, p. 33).

Farmer clarifies the issue at this point by differentiating between a general defining concept and a normative defining concept. In a general defining concept, things are related to one another as various instances of a general type. In a normative defining concept, they are related because they express or approximate to, in varying degrees, an ideal type. If the first concept be used then we fall into two fallacies. One fallacy is that if we define Christianity by its *distinctive* essence, then either Christianity is a true religion and the other religions are not, or Christianity is not a true religion and the others are. The second fallacy is that if we accept that all religions including Christianity belong together and share a common essence, then there is no essential distinction between them, and Christianity loses its distinctness.

Now Farmer uses, instead, the normative defining concept. He points out that this means that entities fall into an ascending ladder of forms as they express the ideal type more adequately. If we adopt this approach and combine with it the insight of Collingwood, then we say that Christianity provides the normative essence, and the other religions differ from it in degree. Yet their differences of degree are so great that Christianity, as the norm, stands apart. The difference of degree merges here into a difference of kind.

To substantiate his position, Farmer suggests that the normative essence of all religions is the personal disclosure of God in Christ. He holds that there is a personal divine self-disclosure in all religions, but they fall short of the norm given in Christianity. To show how great is the difference of degree between them and Christianity, he turns to worship as the area where the normative concept is best defined. Here he finds seven points which are brought to a focus in the normative essence of Christian worship, where man enters most fully into personal relationship with God. These points are: an apprehension of a personal and transcendent Presence; the realized perfection of all values is in this Presence; He comes to us as absolute demand; He comes to us as final succor; He is immanently active in the deeps of the believer's being; He is experienced in the *sui generis* numinous feeling. Farmer finds these points, in varying degrees, in all the world's religions, but only in Christianity do they come together in final and normative form.

We shall here take up Troeltsch's suggestion, for, on the basis of Farmer's description of God as absolute demand and final succor in worship and encounter, the finality of Christianity might be established. We note that the finality lies here in the quality and nature of the divine revelation, and not just in the religious response, for it is the revelation that brings any distinctive qualities to religious behavior. In structure all religious behavior generally manifests similar characteristics. What makes it distinctive is the content given to it by its specific revelation. It is the quality of its claimed revelation of God which gives Christianity finality.

Religions tend to fall into two groups around the themes of absolute demand and final succor, and the groups correspond to the mystical and historical types already discussed. We find the vision of God as inexorable demand in both Judaism and Islam, with their legal formulations. Man's authentic existence comes as he unites his will with the divine in complete obedience. So man has to struggle to remove his alienation by obedience to an absolute demand which he cannot meet. This is the burden of Islam and of Judaism's religion of law. But then there is the other aspect of the divine disclosure—God as final succor, as compassion and grace. This is treasured in the Hindu sects, in the teachings of the Bhagavadgita and of Ramanuja, and in Mahayana Buddhism with its vision of the Buddha as the gracious down-gazing Lord. Yet, in a very real sense, the moral demand is less central, and always in the background, God is beyond good and evil. Man's goal is to escape from the frustrations and sufferings of human existence, not from sin and moral evil. Indeed personal values and individual freedom find little place in these religions. It is only in Christianity that absolute demand and final succor truly meet. For there, in Christ, God is disclosed as he who does not relax the absoluteness of his moral claim on obedience. But he also graciously comes as final succor. He meets those demands himself and offers men a forgiveness which they do not deserve and a redemption which they have not earned. Absolute demand and final succor meet redemptively in the Christian vision of God. God is both a just God and a Savior. He is both a 'consuming fire' and a 'refuge and strength'. This self-disclosure is final and normative!

Tillich likewise looks for the criterion of finality in the quality of the disclosure rather than in that of the response. No response is adequate to what is disclosed, and its religious advocates must bow with all other religious men under the judgment of a final disclosure.

We have only to remember the diversity of contents in the various sects of any specific religion to realize that no religion *per se* can claim to be the norm above all others. But there is a basic disclosure which such a specific religion claims as its distinctive possession, and it is such disclosures that must be adjudged in the pursuit of finality. Those religions which best retain personal values would seem to be more acceptable candidates, and these are constituted by the historical religions—Islam, Judaism, and Christianity. Now each claims disclosures which are mediated through persons. Tillich suggests that the test for finality rests upon the nature of the medium through which the divine disclosure is made. "The bearer of a final revelation must surrender his finitude. . . . not only his life, but also his finite power and knowledge and perfection. In doing so. . . . he becomes completely transparent to the mystery he reveals." (P. Tillich, *Systematic Theology*, Vol. I, Chicago: Chicago University Press, 1951, p. 133). By this Tillich means that only a fully authentic person, completely surrendered to God's will, a truly theonomos man, can mediate a final disclosure of the ultimate Presence. History testifies to such a man in Jesus of Nazareth. He was so surrendered to God that the divine power operated fully in his life. He found his essential freedom in doing the Father's will. In him alienation and estrangement were absent. He was an authentic person, essentially man as man ought to be, and so the divine Presence came shining through his human person and words. This is the miracle of the Incarnation. Here is the final disclosure. It is eschatologically, but not chronologically, final.

In the light of this disclosure, no religion can claim finality, for all our human religious responses, even the best of them, stand under judgment. Our inadequate responses can at best only point to a loving personal Presence as the Ultimate Reality.

The Primacy of the Religious Response to the Universe

We may claim finality for the Christian revelation at the level of the religious response to reality, but can we claim primacy for the religious response *per se* as the interpretative center for the understanding of the universe? We have claimed that, in religion, there is a personal self-disclosure of ultimate reality, but there are other claimants based on other experiences. Can we honestly claim that a religiously based faith-hypothesis is the best approach to understanding our world and for integrating our manifold experiences? If we can, then we may move on with justification to claim finality for the Christian position and its theistic system.

We have seen that all dimensions of experience may also mediate the divine presence and have religious overtones. The moral claims of others upon us may become a divine demand. The glimpse of truth may become a religious experience. The vision of beauty may become a vision of the beauty of holiness. Such experiences can become moments of worship and divine disclosure!

Because all dimensions of experience may mediate a divine disclosure, we have indications of the primacy of religious experience. Polanyi has made us very aware of subsidiary and focal awareness and emphasized the reality of the tacit dimension of knowledge. If we focalize our awareness upon one dimension of experience, there is always present a subsidiary awareness of the other levels of reality. Provided our response has not been violated by some inadequate presupposition which inhibits a full appreciation of the richness of our world, there is a tacit knowledge in the background of our awareness. Thus the aesthetic experience may be colored by religious and moral overtones, and the scientist in the laboratory may have the feelings associated with a religious quest. This serves to reinforce the idea that all our values coalesce in the experience of the holy. It also explains why the religious or numinous feeling in its uniqueness gathers around it 'felt analogies' from other dimensions of experience.

All this points to the primacy of the religious response. It is significant that science, morality and art emerged, in the developing history of the human race, within the aegis of religion. As John Macmurray has pointed out: "religion is at once the oldest and most universal form of human reflection and culture" (Essay on "Religion in Transformation" in *The Changing World*, ed. J. R. R. Brumwell, London: George Rutledge & Sons, 1965, p. 255). We can find no primitive people without some form of religious response, some reverence for what they regard as ultimate and of supreme worth, some pattern of worship. Magic came to birth within this aegis, and out of it slowly, through the devious paths of alchemy and astrology, all tinged with religious colorings, there emerged modern science. And modern science is a quest for truth. It did not arise merely out of curiosity. It involves, at its deepest level, a heuristic passion, even though it has very practical concerns. The same argument applies to the close association of morality with religion in the early existence, side by side, of moral and ritual laws under the aegis of the god, and the still earlier presence of the religiously sanctioned *tabus*. All this would suggest that religion is a response to a Presence in the depth of the universe which embraces all those other aspects of reality with the understanding and pursuit of which morality, science and art are concerned. To cite Macmurray again: "There must be some factor in the human environment to which religion is the response; and since science and art are first developed within religion, it would seem that this factor must somehow embrace and contain the factors to which these more specialized departments of reflective life are directed" (*ibid.*, p. 255).

With such an understanding of the primacy of the religious response and in the light of the finality of the Christian revelation, reason may seek to build a compatible system.

The Place of Reason—
Faith, Proof and Understanding

4 Our discussion of the cognitive dimension of the divine disclosure has already made evident the rational aspect of the religious response. That response, when it is genuine, involves the full personality and is of the nature of commitment or trust. It is a faith attitude in which the religious person commits himself or herself to the self-disclosure of the divine presence. The intuitive insight into ultimate reality which that disclosure offers is expressed in models or analogies which are themselves shaped within the disclosure-situation. In a kind of Jacob's ladder there is a divine human cooperation in the formulation of these models, as the human imagination operates under the guidance of the divine activity. Thus the cognitive reason in the religious response comes into full play. The synthetic aspect of reason, grasping the wholeness of the disclosure, is in the forefront, but the analytical aspect is also present. From the models thus formulated, propositions are shaped to express the content of the disclosure situation. In this way, a group of believers is formed within which the models become central clues and which expresses these models in propositional form. Thereby faith becomes associated with assent or belief, the acceptance of a set of propositions in which the divine disclosure peculiar to the group is formulated.

Such a religious group is not just contemporary with the initial disclosure. As the models and their accompanying propositions are communicated to successive generations, the original disclosure is repeated. The clues so provided point to the disclosure situation, and this becomes contemporaneous within the new historical setting. The original self-giving of God is the permanent point of reference. But as the models which are appropriate to its content and their associated propositions are communicated to successive generations, in proclamation, teaching, ritual and creeds, there is a continuing dependent revelation. What was originally revealed to one individual for his group is actually revealed for all mankind and becomes a dependent revelation as new individuals and groups receive it down historical time. The divine Spirit, working through the clues, illumines the cognitive reason of individual believers, singly or in a group, and brings them into a disclosure-situation in which the original revelation becomes contemporaneous. Both Kierkegaard and Tillich have made this of specific significance in the case of the Christian religion, but it applies to all divine disclosures even though it is specially significant in the case of the historical religions.

Although religion arises through an encounter with the divine Presence in a disclosure-situation and finds its basic response in the total commitment of the personality to the revealed Presence, philosophers have always sought for a rational demonstration of such a faith attitude. Believing in the validity and sufficiency of man's rational processes, philosophical thought has sought to develop arguments for the existence and nature of a Transcendent Reality, quite independent of the specific and focal religious response. Until the last decade Christian apologists, for example, spent considerable time discussing such arguments. In addition, natural theology was regarded as an essential substratum of rational argument upon which a Christian systematic theology could be erected. By natural theology was meant the attempt of the unaided reason, starting with the data provided by the world-consciousness, to arrive by logical processes at the existence of the deity and to indicate those aspects of his nature which reason could attain with no supernatural assistance. Such natural theology has frequently been rejected, for we have recognized that all such attempts have a tacit religious commitment underlying their rational processes. Once we recognize that all reasoning takes place within the aegis of absolute presuppositions or faith-hypotheses to which the thinker is either consciously or tacitly committed, we realize that no rational *proof* can be offered for the religious insight into the heart of reality. We must, however, examine the so-called theistic proofs, and assess their significance, if any, for religious thinking.

Before we proceed to this, the reader will notice that we have used the word 'theistic'. This term, as we defined it in the first chapter, best describes the understanding of God and his relation to the world which is offered by the historical religions of Christianity, Judaism and Islam. We have already sought to establish the finality of the Christian religion, in the sense that the Christian disclosure provides the norm by which all other claimed disclosures must be judged and before which all our human religious responses stand condemned. On this ground, we shall take the religious system of theism both as a basis for insight into ultimate reality and as a basis for understanding ourselves and our world. At the same time we must examine rival systems of thought, religious and secular, both as to adequacy for dealing with crucial issues of thought and experience and as to positive contributions by which they augment or challenge the insights of a theistic approach.

Theism and the Judaeo-Christian Understanding of God

Theism as a philosophical system has arisen in our Western civilization and shows strong marks of the influence of the Judaeo-Christian tradition. It is indeed a de-Christianized form of the world-view offered by the Christian faith. Its understanding of the deity and of the relation of God to the world is identical with that of the Christian community with specifically Christian references omitted. Since we are assuming it as the normative philosophical system in this sense, we need to clarify its understanding of God.

The Judaeo-Christian tradition emerged in the ancient Near East among the Hebrew people as a monotheistic faith. Ultimate reality is One, and the many are derived from the One, to put this idea in its philosophical form. In religious parlance, there is only one God, the supreme and ultimate Being upon whom all things depend and from whom they derive their being. In the historic words of the Hebrew confession: "Hear, O Israel: The Lord our God is one Lord; and you shall love the Lord your God with all your heart, and with all your soul, and with all your might." Other people might be polytheists and worship many gods, but the Hebrews believed in one God. Moreover they were not *henotheists*, allowing that there might be many gods, but giving their allegiance to only one of them, Yahweh of Horeb/Sinai and the Exodus deliverance. They were *monotheists*, believing in one God and serving only him. That tradition was continued in the Christian community which never allowed its trinitarian understanding of God to degenerate into tritheism. The God and Father of the Lord Jesus Christ is the supreme reality, the ruler of the universe and the God of all peoples. Jesus Christ is himself God incarnate, not other than God, but the one God fully present in human flesh in his eternal mode of being as Son. Theism takes this affirmation of monotheism, omits specifically Christian and Jewish references, and describes the ultimate Reality as one Supreme Being who controls and sustains the whole universe and the whole process of human history. There is, of course, underlying it a tacit acceptance of the Judaeo-Christian understanding of God.

Such theism regards God as personal, regarding the human personality as a basic model for understanding the nature of the divine presence. It rejects any suggestion that God is less than personal, a blind, chaotic, groping life-force, a naturalistic urge. Equally it rejects the idea of God as impersonal. It is, however, ready to accept a view of God as supra-personal in the sense that he is at least personal in his dealings with men and the world, although there is a mysterious transcendence in him which points to a depth for which a personal model is inadequate. Yet whatever be the mystery, it does not contradict our personal understanding of his presence and activity in our world. Both philosophically and theologically it is inappropriate to describe God as a Person. Rather the appropriate description is the use of the adjective personal. He is personal Being. The highest model available in human experience is a personal one, but even this is only analogy. God, in his mystery, transcends all our attempts to probe the depths of his being. Furthermore, he is not a Person in the sense of being one among many. He is the ground of being, from which all beings derive their existence and by which they are sustained. Thus we can understand those who like Tillich regard the verb 'exist' as inapplicable to God, for the description 'existence' cannot be applied to him as it is used for us finite beings and our world. All existing beings have their source and ground in him, and thus his being is transcendent to and other than theirs. Yet it is difficult to find any more adequate description than God existing, provided we recognize the distinction just made.

The emphasis on the divine transcendence and otherness is not only a reminder that our models are analogical and must not be taken literally. Whatever God's 'Thouness', to use Buber's description, is in its depths, it is an infinite 'Thouness' and an unoriginated 'Thouness'. God is the sole ultimate reality, dependent upon no other for his being. He is sufficient in himself. He lives from himself. He is self-existent. The technical term used for this by the medieval philosophers was *aseity*. He owes his being to nothing beyond himself. God is 'He who is'. In the phrases already used in this book, he is the Unconditioned, the Ultimate Reality. Beyond him there is no other.

He has then no beginning and no ending. He is eternal. Immediately we face the vexed issue of time and eternity. The theist understands that in his transcendence, God is above time, yet the Judaeo-Christian understanding of God as a living God, as God who acts, a God who wills and whose purpose is being fulfilled in his world, means that eternity must include time. If we may speak of God as experiencing, we mean that God does experience time, but not as we finite persons do. His eternity is not unending time, for there can be no before and after with him as there is with us. Equally it is not totally other than time, for then our human existence and the processes of history and nature would mean nothing to him. Because theism tacitly accepts the Judaeo-Christian understanding of God, it must therefore accept that, for a personal deity, time is meaningful, even though God transcends its flow. Sometimes thinkers suggest that, for God, all temporal events are gathered up as elements in a completed purpose and that from his eternal stance God surveys and experiences all our times in his eternal now. We shall return to this later. It is enough here to stress God's otherness, and yet we must also remember his nearness.

Immediately we face the theistic understanding of God as Creator. Once more there is a tacit acceptance of the revelatory insights in the Judaeo-Christian tradition. The world and human beings exist by the creative activity of a personal God. They have been posited by him, called into being by his divine fiat, out of nothing. This concept of creation out of nothing, *creatio ex nihilo*, indicates the use of a model or analogy taken from human creativity but adding as a qualifier that

God was not using preexistent stuff to initiate his creative act. Thereby we are reminded that God's creative activity is both like and unlike that of his creatures. He works with no material which exists totally independent of himself. 'All that is' is derived from him. Furthermore, it is not derived from his own substance. Thereby theism rejects any pantheistic references. The world is not divine nor have human beings 'sparks of the divine' in them. 'All that is' is not God. Equally, although it is derived from God, it comes into being by a personal act of his creative will. He wills that it should be and calls it into being 'out of nothing'. No attempt at questionable subterfuge can evade this irrationality, at least at our human level of thinking. God is *absolute* Creator.

Thereby everything is dependent, totally dependent, upon the Creator. Indeed, it exists by his creative activity and it persists by his sustaining power. He alone keeps it in being above the abyss of nothingness out of which it has been called by his creative act. Thus there is a continuing creation. The world was not called into being and then left to its own devices. Rather it continues to be, because the creative will sustains those energies which make its continuity possible and guides them so that the creatively new may emerge within the process.

God is transcendent in his innermost being, but his activity as Creator as well as his revelatory activity point to an immanence within his creation. He is thus both beyond and within the movements of nature and of history. Also, he is both transcendent to finite human beings and yet immanently active in the depth of their being, as we have already suggested.

Yet the theist would never allow such an emphasis on the divine immanence to suggest that there is an element of deity, a divine dimension, in the created order itself. The 'creation out of nothing' safeguards against any suggestion that the creatures have deity within themselves or that they can themselves and of themselves become in any way divine. Always God is God and alone God, and his creatures remain creatures. Between the two there is a divide fixed. As we have indicated earlier, such theism rules out any thought of *panentheism*, if this term indicates creation by emanation from the divine substance. Yet, allowing for the *creatio ex nihilo* stipulation, the theist does not hold that the whole created order lives and moves and has its being in

God. The Transcendent Deity is also an Immanent Presence in his world.

We have already examined the various aspects of the divine disclosure as these are celebrated in religious worship, and we have noted that the Christian disclosure meets all these requirements most fully. So far our theistic approach to God has followed closely this series of requirements. We turn now to the pair of requirements which we found to be crucial in establishing finality for the Christian disclosure—a personal God who encounters men in absolute demand and final succor. Grounded in Otto's analysis of the religious experience of the Holy and brought to a focus in the divine disclosures associated with the Judaeo-Christian tradition, this dual aspect of the divine Presence is a significant element in the theistic understanding of God. God is both morally righteous and self-giving love. He is both the enthronement of our moral values and the actuality of love. Again we can see the tacit influence of the Christian disclosure upon ethical theism, for love in the Christian sense has a different connotation from its meaning in Greek thought. The Greek concept of love, enshrined in *eros*, was directed only to what was worth loving. But the Christian revelation, brought to a focus in Jesus Christ, manifested a love which gave and spent itself; a love, also, which was directed to the unlovely and made them of worth; indeed, a love which was creative and redemptive. Because such a meaning could not be carried by *eros* and its cognates, the early Christians coined the word *agape* to describe the essential Christian disclosure of God's nature and activity. God is love; but it is this kind of love—redemptive, creative, self-giving.

Yet if God is love, he is also morally righteous. He is supremely attractive, but he is also absolutely demanding. Righteousness describes that inner integrity in which God is always true to himself. This means that he demands of men the kind of conduct which is consonant with his own being and purpose of love. Hence Jesus could declare that the core of moral behavior was loving God with one's whole being and one's neighbor as oneself. Only so can a man be described as morally good, and the norm for such moral goodness is enthroned in the heart of the universe. God is morally righteous, and such goodness must be understood in terms of his essential being as love.

This means also that God is judgmental and that his 'wrath' is a reality. Yet that 'wrath' is the underside of his love. He has created a moral universe, in which the rejection of his demands brings, in the end, disaster, both personally and socially. Yet always his last word is redemptive, for the judgmental aspect of God's activity is disciplinary, aiming at attaining the goal set by reconciling and self-giving love.

Such a theistic understanding of God is grounded in a faith commitment. It is certainly not self-evident, although a man may be guided to such a conviction by clues which have their origin in religious disclosure. Reason, in the sense of analytical, discursive reasoning, may get to work on such a basis and seek to establish a coherent view of the universe and a satisfying understanding of human personality and freedom. Yet reason always seeks more than this, namely to establish logically the actuality of that divine being without whose reality the theistic worldview has no *raison d'etre*. We have already indicated the fallacy in this position and in any attempt to establish a theistic position by a natural theology based on man's "unaided reason." We must now examine these various attempts of reason to by-pass faith and formulate 'proofs' of the divine existence.

From Faith to Proof—The Value, if Any, of the Theistic Arguments

These so-called 'proofs' fall into four approaches—the *ontological*, the *cosmological*, the *teleological*, and the *moral*. Claiming to be logical they all fail at just this crucial point, for all manifest illogicalities. This might be expected, for, if the existence and nature of God were beyond logical dispute, much of the evil in our world would never have arisen and doubts would soon disappear. Yet despite their failure as logical arguments and thus as proofs of the divine existence, we can find value in them besides the obvious reminder that faith in the invisible and infinite Being can never be replaced by logical demonstration.

To the 'proofs', the division of religious philosophy into ontological and cosmological types is very applicable. The first is appropriate to the ontologistic approach since it begins with human self-consciousness and its contents. The second and third fall into the cosmological approach to reality. The fourth and moral argument is more difficult to classify, but fundamentally it falls into the ontological approach.

The first formulation of the *Ontological Argument* was by Anselm, the Archbishop of Canterbury (1033-1109 A.D.). Greatly influenced by the thought of St. Augustine, Anselm was an ontologist, believing in the immanent presence of God illuminating the mind. Thus he believed that the mind has an *a priori* awareness of the divine presence and that the concepts of the mind are divinely informed so that they correspond to objective reality. When we remember this, we can understand the structure of his ontological argument.

Anselm began by attacking the blindness of the fool who denies the reality of God. For actually, according to Anselm's ontologism, he does possess a knowledge of God even though he does not recognize it. Every man understands what he means when he uses the idea 'God', even though he denies him. But if he knows the essence of God, he cannot deny God's existence, for God's existence is contained in his essence. This statement Anselm proceeds to demonstrate logically. Thus really his argument is an attempt to give a rational demonstration of an intuitive awareness. It is significant that in his *Proslogium*, Anselm includes the argument in a prayer to that God whose existence he is attempting to prove!

He holds that all men accept the idea of "the Being than which no greater can be conceived," the concept of God. But a being existing in the mind as a concept does not necessarily exist outside the mind as a fact. At this point Anselm introduces a premise which is really the Achilles heel of his argument—what exists in actuality is superior to what is only an idea in the mind. Now, so far as finite things are concerned, this premise does not necessarily imply their existence. This is not the case, however, when we consider the concept of an infinite and perfect Being than whom no greater can be thought. For if such a Being be only a concept in the mind, a greater than it can be thought, namely such a Being existing both in the mind and in actuality. But since God is the Being than whom no greater can be conceived, he must exist extra-mentally as well as mentally, in reality as well as in concept. To think of a being greater than God is to think of a being greater than the greatest being that reason can conceive. This is evidently self-contradictory. So God exists. By the very definition which Anselm gives to God, God must exist, for his existence is implied in his essence.

Anselm was at least trying to deal with Transcendence, for he is defining God as the limit of our finite conceiving. His argument is, however, open to serious criticism, yet we must delay this and deal first with the attempt of Descartes to reformulate the argument. Descartes, too, stood in the Augustinian tradition and was an ontologist, but he carried this position to its extreme. Like all ontologists he looked for rationally guaranteed certainties, and he found that he could doubt all the statements he made about his experience at all levels. There was always the possibility of error, especially at the level of sense experience. In his search for one indubitable statement, Descartes arrived at his own thinking process. Although every assertion was open to doubt, the one thing he could not doubt was that he himself was doubting. So he asserted what he believed to be indubitably true— *cogito ergo sum*, 'I think, therefore I am'. He concluded that what made it so certain was that it could be conceived so clearly and distinctly. From this it was a logical step to assert that all other statements which are clear and distinct might likewise be indubitable. Now among such ideas, the idea of perfection conjoined to existence stood out clearly and distinctly in Descartes' mind. Hence he concluded that the supremely perfect Being must exist. Thus Descartes very specifically assumes that existence is a quality or predicate or attribute which can help to define an essence. In the case of the supremely perfect Being, he contends that it is a necessary attribute of the divine essence. It helps to define the essential nature of God, so that God's existence may be inferred from his essence, just as with finite things their characteristic properties may be inferred from their essence. The triangularity of a triangle, for instance, is such that the properties of triangularity may be inferred from it. They are defining predicates. This assumption of Descartes, present also in Anselm's thought, is the obvious Achilles' heel of the ontological argument, as we shall see shortly.

Based on this assumption Anselm provided an answer to his contemporary critic Gaunilo. The latter used the figure of an island and its existence. Only exploration can assure us that the idea of an island in the mind really exists *de facto*. The mere idea does not prove that there is an objective reality corresponding to it. Several hundred years later, Kant brought the same kind of criticism against Descartes. He used the idea of a hundred guilders in the pocket. The only proof of their existence is to produce them. We cannot argue from the logical necessity of an idea to its actual existence in fact.

Anselm's answer to Gaunilo was that the latter's objection held of finite and sensible things, but that he was not talking about such objects. God is not a finite object in space/time and subject to sense experience. If he were, he would not be the greatest being that can be conceived. Anselm's argument applies only to such a being, God, and not to sensible things. Now in this sense Anselm is right. Arguments applicable to finite things do not apply to transcendence. But then how does he know that his argument applies there, especially if the argument itself has a logical fallacy?

One aspect of this fallacy lies in the assumption that existence is a predicate. Existence is not a defining predicate. Kant made much of this in his criticism of Descartes' argument. We can draw out this position more clearly if we note that two kinds of statements can be made about any finite thing—one is a statement which includes defining attributes or predicates, and the other is a statement that the thing exists. For instance, we may say that "hobbits are of small stature and live underground." This would define a hobbit. It is quite different from the assertion: "Hobbits exist." The latter statement makes no difference to what the hobbit essentially is. Usually, of course, statements of the first kind require statements of the second kind; otherwise they are imaginative and non-factual. But they may be made in this way, and then the first kind of statement is non-verifiable and non-sensical. Now the trouble with the ontological argument is that it treats 'existence' as an attribute or predicate. Hence the argument moves from a Being who has the attributes of supreme power, perfect knowledge, but not of existence to one who has omnipotence and omniscience but also existence. But if existence is not an attribute, then existence or non-existence will make no difference to the quality of perfection. This may be present in the imagination, but the fact that it is at the limit of such imaginative conceiving contributes nothing to its actual existence. As with 'hobbits' so with God, at this level of argument!

The deeper aspect of this logical fallacy lies in its confusion of kinds of statement, and we need to remember here that we are talking about assertions and not beings. There are contingent statements and necessary statements. Contingent statements may be true or false according to verification in actual fact. A denial of such a statement would not involve a contradiction. Thus the assertion: "Some cows produce milk" is a contingent statement. All statements which are factual are contingent, and this would include all assertions that something exists. On the other hand, a necessary statement is one which cannot be denied without involving a contradiction. Here the statement "Either some cows produce milk or none do" is a necessary statement. Such a statement depends only on the meaning of the terms involved in the statement. It is non-factual. Now if we make a statement and treat it as both necessary and contingent, we are evidently being illogical. For such an assertion would then be both deniable without contradiction and deniable with contradiction, both factual and non-factual.

When we turn to the ontological argument, the illogicality involved is quite clear. It seeks to make the statement that 'God exists', a statement which can be denied and which is thus contingent. Yet it also seeks to make the statement necessary by its definition of God in which for a supreme being existence and essence belong together, a statement that is undeniable by the definition.

The value of the ontological argument lies solely in its attempt to state rationally, even though it fails here, the assertion of faith that God *is*. Its failure is a warning that all faith assertions are open to doubt and that no indubitable statement about ultimate reality is possible. The Transcendent is always beyond our logic, and all that arguments like this can do is point to a possibility. To make existence a defining predicate, at least in the case of God, is to make a contingent statement about God into a necessary statement. Logic breaks at this point, but the so-called argument may yet point to the mystery of Transcendence.

The cosmological approach to ultimate reality involves us in two arguments. The first is the cosmological argument based on the concept of cause, and the second is the teleological argument concerned with the idea of design. To consider the *Cosmological Argument* first, we need to remember that it has a long history, going back to its initial formulation by Aristotle. It became important in the medieval period when Thomas Aquinas made it basic in his construction of a natural theology. Fundamentally it is based on the Aristotelian syllogism

Every event has a cause (Major Premise)

The universe is an event (Minor Premise)
Therefore the universe has a cause (Conclusion)
That cause is itself uncaused and such an
uncaused cause is what we mean by 'God'.

Aquinas gave three forms of the argument, and the second and third forms or 'ways' are the more significant. The second way is really that outlined in the above syllogism, as was Aristotle's original formulation of the argument. It is concerned with the idea of a first or final cause. Every event in our experience is caused by something else, but the latter cause is, in its turn, also caused, and so we have a continuing regress of causes. This series could go on *ad infinitum*, but Aquinas felt that such an infinite regress would be repugnant to the reason. Hence there must be a first cause which is itself uncaused, an uncaused cause, an unmoved mover, which we call God. In this way we arrive at a being who is sufficient in itself, a necessary being in the sense that it does not depend upon any other being for its existence.

The third way of Aquinas is a more appealing statement and was taken up by Leibnitz. It is the cosmological argument proper. It is concerned with contingent and necessary being. Contingent beings exist because some being, other than themselves, brought them into existence. There is, therefore, the element of contingency or possibility about them, for they might not have existed and their actuality depends upon some other being that made their existence possible. Now all things which we experience in our world, including ourselves and all other persons, are contingent in this sense. They are dependent and derived beings. We have already defined a necessary being as one that is sufficient in itself. But if all things exist because they are derived from and depend upon other things, then there is no final explanation of the whole system. We are left with an irrational and chaotic state of affairs in which all is contingent and in which only partial explanations are available by reference to the other contingent beings upon which any particular being depends. Therefore there must be a necessary being which constitutes the ultimate ground of all contingent beings. As Leibnitz expressed it, there must be a 'sufficient reason' outside the series of contingent things, a being which carries in itself both the reason for its own existence and the final reason for the existence of all contingent beings. If this were not so, we should have no ultimate reason at which to end. This necessary being we call God.

We note, at the outset, certain differences between this kind of argument and the preceding ontological argument. For one thing, the ontological argument moves from a contingent statement to a necessary statement, whereas this argument moves from contingent being to necessary being. This argument is not open, as some critics have suggested, to a misuse of the word 'necessary'. In one sense necessary may mean *logically* necessary, then it applies to statements or propositions, as in the ontological argument. But in the cosmological argument, it does not bear this connotation. 'Necessary being' is not *logically* necessary being, which would, of course, be unintelligible usage of necessary. Rather, it is concerned with a factual or existential necessity, self-sufficiency or 'total being-from-selfness'. Hence the description of God as a necessary being by no means implies that the proposition 'God exists' is a logically necessary truth. Thereby the cosmological argument is not concerned to show that the existence of God is undeniable, so that even the fool really knows in his heart that God exists. Rather, it is satisfied to demonstrate, to its own satisfaction, that God does exist.

A second point of contrast is that the ontological argument is concerned with God as the most perfect being, whereas the cosmological argument thinks of God as necessary being. The real issue then becomes whether such a necessary being exists, so we turn to a criticism of this so-called argument. We shall find that, like the ontological argument, it has its logical fallacy.

The argument to a First Cause might seem to have support from the current scientific theory about the origin at the universe. The view increasingly favored is the so-called 'Big Bang' theory which postulates the origin of the universe as a vast explosion of energy about ten million years ago and a consequent expansion of the whole cosmic system. In any case, the argument that an infinitive regress is repugnant to the reason has been supported by science itself, and the cosmological argument might seem to have some basis in the scientific world-view. Even so, there is no justification for building too much on this, since rival theories, such as that of a pulsating universe, cannot be ruled out. The origination of the present universe must not be identified with the origination of the physical order, even though it does appear that any attempt to move into and behind the cosmic explosion is impossible.

Much more relevant to and also critical of this form of the argument is its use of the word 'cause'. First of all, ever since Hume, the idea of cause has been called in question in various ways. Hume himself reduced causation to the conjunction of cause and effect in our experience of them. Thus, if we say that event A was caused by event B, Hume would say that we are stating that, in our experience, we never observe event A without its being preceded by event B. Sequence in time is really what we mean when we talk about causation. But then Kant took another line and held that the human mind projects the category of causation upon reality so that the causative relationship is within the sensing structure of the consciousness. On these bases, the argument is ruled out. Modern science also makes the argument invalid, since the so-called causal laws are no longer regarded as regulative in nature but rather as statistical averages describing the high probabilities of such regularities of natural behavior. Thus scientific positivism has taken up the heritage of Hume.

In any case, the argument fails even if a causative structure is accepted, for the idea of 'cause' results from human observation of an effect and a cause. Thus both terms in a causal relationship have to be observable for it to be asserted. But 'the universe' is hardly an 'observable' for finite human minds, and 'God' is certainly not an 'observable' by definition. So the idea of a causal relationship between God and the world is not a possibility. Our logic breaks down. Furthermore, it breaks down logically, not only because we are using the word 'cause' outside the aegis where it applies, but also because we are further speaking about an 'uncaused cause.' We are giving 'cause' a new meaning which has no justification in the empirical area in which the idea of 'cause' arises.

This form of the argument thus fails logically. Actually it is not an argument but an analogical application of the idea of 'cause' to the relation of God to his world. It does not prove that God exists; but it does help us to make our experience of the world and nature more intelligible by using an analogy, taken from the natural order, to explain the relation of God to the world. In this sense it is merely a rationalization of the religious understanding of creation and is convincing only to those who believe already in God the Creator.

The second and more acceptable form of the argument turns upon the idea of a necessary being in contrast to the contingent beings of intramundane experience. It is open to like attack, for the 'uncaused cause' is another way of speaking about necessary being. The argument points to a ground of being upon which all the contingent beings of the world depend and from which they derive their being. Its thesis is that without such a necessary ground, the world and its beings are not intelligible.

Now this is the crux of the matter. The alternatives are clear—either the world is intelligible only if it is grounded in a necessary being or it is intelligible without such grounding. Just at this point the argument fails to carry conviction, for there are many who would contend that the contingent things of the world are completely intelligible within the scientific context in which they are situated. Furthermore, such a scientific context may need to be explained in a wider and like context, but one can go on widening the scope of reference *ad infinitum* and intelligibility will always be present. It is true that science is increasingly becoming aware of mystery, but there is always present the conviction that such areas will sooner or later yield up their secrets and become scientifically intelligible.

Such scientific skeptics might even argue, and they do, that scientific intelligibility by no means implies that the universe is not ultimately unintelligible. It may well be just brute actuality, a chaotic mass, in which science is carving out an area of intelligibility. In that case, to talk about a necessary ground of being is meaningless. The universe has no meaning.

Now it is just here that the attack of the critics needs to be ameliorated to some degree, for advocates of the argument would contend that they are not talking about scientific explanation but about final intelligibility. They are concerned not with explaining why certain contingent things exist, but with why there is something and not nothing, why there is anything at all. This final meaning must lie beyond the universe itself. The scientific skeptics are actually making the physical universe all that is and treating it as necessary being. All the parts of the universe are scientifically explicable within this physical whole, but the universe itself is inexplicable. It just *is*, hard brute fact! For them the expression 'necessary being' is meaningless, but so is their physical universe! This does not, however, remove the option that the argument offers.

The option is not helped by the criticisms already made in the case of the 'first cause' form of the argument. 'Necessary being' has no empirical referent. All we experience are contingent beings. All the argument, in this form, really does is to express in rational form the feeling we have that there is 'Something', the 'Unconditioned', without which we should not be. It points to a ground of being and leaves it there. Such a ground of reality escapes all description, since it has no empirical referent. It is a pure assumption to identify such a ground of being with the Christian God. So to describe it gives it a Christian setting, but then to affirm 'necessary being' at all implies this or, at least, a religious presupposition. The argument turns upon the ultimate intelligibility, the final rationality, of the universe, but this too is a religious affirmation. The critic and the scientific skeptic who do not accept this and its definition of intelligibility will not find the argument convincing.

The third argument is the *Teleological*. It is based upon the idea of design. Its fundamental contention is that the universe must be viewed as somewhat like a highly complex mechanism and thus as the product of a designing mind. Plato used the argument in the *Timaeus*. He contended that the principle that "the mind orders all things" is the only one worthy of the world around us and the heavens above us. It was used by Aquinas and included in his five ways. It was not, however, until the 18th century that the argument came into its own and achieved its height of popularity. As adumbrated by Paley in his *Natural Theology*, it became the foundation of the deistic view of God. Paley likened the universe to a watch, the design of which involves a designer, man. Hence, he argued, "by way of analogy, the abundant evidence of design in the world, proves that it must have a designer, and that designer must, and can be no other than God." Many of his contemporaries carried the idea to extremes, seeking for all kinds of natural phenomena, the utilitarian adaptations of which demonstrated the purpose for which they had been created. This cheap salesmanship of a designer God reached its nadir when one brilliant(!) mind contended that the Creator had created cork trees to provide stoppers for wine bottles! Others argued that vermin infested the human body in order to provoke cleanliness.

Paley, in a much more sober way, pointed to the orderly rotation of the planets, the regularity of the seasons of this earth, the coordinated functioning of the human brain despite its complex cellular structure, the marvelous adaptability and mechanism of the human eye, and so on. He did not feel that such harmonious and well-formed aspects of nature could result from random forces of nature. Rather they pointed to a great and good God.

We need to note, first of all, that the position of Paley and other thinkers reflects the deism prevalent in the eighteenth century. This immediately weakens the argument in modern eyes, for it regards God as so transcendent that the world is controlled like a vast machine by the laws which he has imposed upon it, and it frowns upon any divine and miraculous intervention in this mechanistic structure. The cogs, wheels, and levers of the vast world-machine run with machinelike regularity and God sits in solitary splendor above the whole structure. It is true that such thinkers still believed in human freedom and morality and found a place for human reason and inventiveness, but thereby they introduced a strange dichotomy into their world structure. They had no place for the divine immanence or an immanent teleology. The teleology was imposed from without. As such it had to be proved as perfect as possible.

Hume seized upon the latter and pointed out the presence of dysteleogical elements in the universe. The presence of evil still remains a serious challenge to the somewhat optimistic note that the teleogical argument manifests, even when an immanent teleogical motif takes the place of the deistic viewpoint of Paley and his contemporaries. Nature does have another face, besides the benevolent aspect which they emphasized. It is cruel and brutal. Its forces can be devastating and destructive. Storms and earthquakes, floods and tornadoes wreak their havoc. There are signs of beauty but also signs of ugliness. Harmony is contrasted with a lack of harmony. Nature is not always well-adapted. It is "red in tooth and claw with ravine," as Tennyson saw. Such poets who have praised nature for its beauty have also been beset by doubts when they confront its wastage. The problem of evil presses heavily on the validity of the teleological argument. If the latter is to have any logical validity at this point, we might infer a dualism and postulate two divine powers, one good and one evil, locked together in cosmic conflict. Christian thinking, with its radical monotheism, certainly cannot rely too heavily on this kind of argument, for it has to take the reality of evil seriously.

Hume, however, brought other criticisms of the argument which also remain valid. For one thing, the appearance of design, of harmony and order, does not necessarily imply an intelligence which is responsible for the design. This criticism has been made more potent by the work of Darwin and by the developments in the evolutionary aspect of biological science. Hume argued that a universe consisting of many diverse parts would, in the course of time, manifest signs of adaptation and harmony if life was to persist in a relatively fixed kind of environment. It would then give the appearance of design, even though it may have originated in a somewhat random and chaotic state of affairs. Order might thus appear in ways other than through conscious planning. He cited the Epicurean model of a universe, consisting of a finite number of particles in random motion. Provided there was unlimited time, such a chaotic assembly might pass through all possible combinations and one of these might perchance appear with stability enough to persist and sustain its structural order of relations between the particles. Our own universe might result in just this way.

Such a possibility became much more plausible after Darwin's theory of evolution by natural selection appeared upon the scene. Here is a possible modification of the Epicurean hypothesis, with real biological evidence to support it. Let us, at once, add that such an interpretation of the evolutionary process is by no means the only one and that a theistic and creative approach to Darwin's hypothesis and its successors is also a very real option! Darwin, however, introduced the idea of small chance variations in the animal order which were weeded out by natural selection, so that only those most fitted to the environment would survive and propagate progeny. His theory has been modified to meet the growing knowledge of biological heredity and genetic structures, but, in its Neo-Darwinian form, the emphasis still falls on random mutations and natural selection. Adaptation to and harmony with the environment are factors in the emergence of new species, and there is an element of randomness in the way in which such changes or new structures emerge in the process. Only those mutated forms capable of surviving in a changing environment persist in the struggle for life. Such a naturalistic interpretation of the Darwinian hypothesis replaces a divine designer by the random forces of nature. It certainly presents an alternative option to the argument from design. Design and order may have come because accidental collocations of natural forces produced ordered structures which had survival value.

There is, however, a more serious criticism of the teleological argument. So long as we are dealing with familiar objects like watches which we know are made by watchmakers, we have a basis on which to make an inference from such an object to its maker or designer. But when we move to the universe the same kind of criticism applies as the one we used in the case of the cosmological argument. The universe is a unique and isolated case. What applies to individual things does not necessarily hold for the whole. We have nothing with which to compare the universe, and so we have no basis for making an inference such as we can make in the case of individual objects. The latter belong to classes, and any inference we draw has a basis in other instances of the same class. Immediately we are face to face with the logical invalidity of the argument. We have no basis for applying to the whole universe what may hold of constituent elements in the universe.

The argument must not be totally dismissed, for it does point to the possibility of an Intelligent Designer. But let us note that, even then, such a Designer is not necessarily the Christian God. For one thing, there is no hint that such a Designer also creates the material. He may be dealing with uncreated material, even refractory material, and then we have a basic dualism. We certainly should not have the Omnipotent Deity of the Judaeo/Christian tradition. Kant pointed out that all the argument can possibly prove is "an Architect of the world, Who is very much limited by the adaptability of the material with which He works, but *not of a Creator of the world*, to whom all things are subject. . . ."

The reference of Hume to the Epicurean hypothesis and the atomic theories of Greeks like Euripides and Lucretius, and the new understandings of the world made possible by the Darwinian theory of biological evolution and the 'big bang' theory of an expanding universe might support the possibility of a whole which begins in a chaotic and random assembly. There is, however, another option when the validity of such theories is accepted, as it increasingly is. This option is to understand God as both transcendent and immanent, creatively present within as well as beyond the process. In that case, we have an immanent teleology rather than one imposed from without by a deistic God. Such a view certainly does not make the argument more valid, but it does offer a more viable religious understanding of the element of design in the universe. The latter is one reason why thinkers who dismiss the argument on logical grounds are still impressed by it. Even Hume, the skeptic, felt that "a purpose, an intention, a design, strikes everywhere the most careless and stupid thinker."

There is a feeling of the presence of God in nature, and the argument puts this impression into words. It is really a rational formulation of the revelation through creation. Apart from such a faith presupposition, the argument really has little value. It only has significance for one who believes in a creator God already and is aware of his revelatory presence in the natural order.

The last argument to be considered is the *Moral Argument*. After Kant had demolished the other three arguments, he sought for another approach to the transcendent Presence. Because he accepted the contemporary deism and had no place for revelation, he sought a base in man's moral experience. Emphasizing the human feeling of ethical compulsion, oughtness, Kant found all men to be subject to an unconditional claim, the categorical imperative expressed in the recognition of duty. He regarded this inescapable sense of duty as the most obvious fact. Such duty is directed to achieving man's highest good, and such a highest good is compounded of virtue and happiness, the consciousness of fulfilling a right act with the accompanying satisfaction of the desire to be happy. Such a *summun bonum*, a union of divergent goals, is only possible if we postulate God as the guarantor that holiness and happiness shall be matched.

Kant's formulation has as ingredient in it his differentiation between reality and appearance, the noumenal and the phenomenal, to which respectively holiness or virtue and happiness belong. A better way of expressing his argument is to replace this dichotomy by the reality of two orders of living—the natural and the moral. The demands of the moral consciousness are directed to man's highest good, but for this to be attained, the natural order must serve the ends of the ethical and spiritual. Now there is always a tension between the natural and the moral, and such a tension can be resolved only by the postulate of a moral God who is both the ground of both orders and the guarantor of their final harmony.

The argument may take another form. In this form there is an attempt to establish the objective reality of moral values and, from such an objectivity, to infer a Transcendent Author. Thus an objective moral law logically implies a divine Law-Giver, and an objective structure of moral values points logically to a Ground of Values.

Rashdall has taken this approach. He regards the feeling of oughtness or moral obligation as universal in the human race, even though the standards of such morality may vary with the social structures and degree of civilized life involved. He further contends, like Kant, that such a feeling is not the same as that associated with acting for personal pleasure or acting for social approval. Duty is right whatever be the consequences, and this suggests that there is an objective moral law independent of any man's likes and desires. If there be such a moral law, man's moral nature is grounded in reality, and this implies a moral Being who transcends the world and is the ground of our moral values, for morality is actual only with mind.

This kind of argument is not convincing to the skeptic, for he can find naturalistic explanations which he regards as satisfactory. By reducing morality to the level of a natural phenomenon, he can claim to remove the tension between the moral and natural orders and to eliminate any idea of the objectivity of ethical values. Thus, he can explain moral behavior at the naturalistic level by identifying it as the kind of activity which has best enabled the human race to survive in the struggle for existence. Such behavior had survival value. Or, again, ethical values and the sense of duty can be ascribed to social pressure and group approval. Morality has a social origin. Actually the two explanations interlock and both claim to offer a viable explanation for the variation of moral standards across the history of the human race. Such views can be countered by the evident fact that moral values in certain situations do not offer survival value, but rather require sacrifice and death. They certainly go often against the pressure of the group. There is, indeed, a real difference between the authority of moral laws and the pressure of social custom and *mores*. Even so, the existence of moral behavior is by no means a convincing base for inferring the reality of God.

As with the other so-called proofs, the moral argument points to the possibility of God. It is really an attempt to offer a rational demonstration of the fact that the moral law is immanent in man's nature and is experienced by the religious man as the voice of God. The truth is that, in the categorical imperative, we are directly in relation to

God. The argument to infer his existence is simply a rationalization of such a faith-stance.

At the end of this long discussion of the theistic arguments, we are left with probability at the best. Logical validity has been shown to be absent, and thereby any cogency disappears. To one who believes already they have value as confirming him in his faith-stance. They might point some to the possibility of God and make a faith-stance more credible. But generally their lack of logical validity vitiates their apologetic value. They do, however, in various ways, emphasize the feeling men have that there is 'something more' than things visible, that there is a 'depth' in our world which would help to unravel the mysteries in our experience. The very fact that we talk about God and have religious feelings and moral obligations gives some validity to man's thinking, however imperfect, along the lines of these arguments.

Believing and Understanding

Once more we return to our original contention that belief in God does not depend upon proofs. Rather it is a matter of insight, which the operation of reason may help to confirm. The analytical reason proceeds to develop and make intelligible that pattern in reality which the synthetic reason or intuitive insight has grasped. Thus the cognitive insight of faith is really the premise rather than the conclusion of the kind of arguments that we have been considering. This is, indeed, the function of the analytical reason, for its task is to make our religious insights into reality intelligible and confirm our belief that they provide a key to understanding the universe and our own lives.

Faith can never remain quiescent. Its cognitive insights need to be expanded and related to every aspect of human experience. Faith has to go in search of understanding, and so Anselm could speak of *fides quaerens intellectum*. As Anselm saw it, we do not, in the last resort, reason in order that we may believe. Rather, we believe in order that we may understand—*credo ut intelligum*. For this medieval thinker and many others who stand in the Augustinian tradition, Christian philosophizing becomes faith seeking to understand itself and its world. The Augustinian paradox is that faith must precede philosophical inquiry. Mere rationalism can originate nothing, for reason depends for its material upon a higher mode of experience (*vide* W. H. V. Read's judgment on Anselm's approach in *Cambridge Medieval History*, V, p. 793).

In thus seeking understanding, faith is also confirmed. For the reason seeks to embrace all of human experience within the aegis of the faith presupposition. Thus the theistic understanding of ultimate reality will embrace both our knowledge of ourselves and our world and also seek to penetrate the areas of mystery which form the penumbra of our experience of our world. There is a shadowed side of our world which our human and natural sciences cannot penetrate. Here, as Gabriel Marcel has indicated, we are not dealing with problems which sooner or later our human methodologies and rational ingenuities will solve. We are dealing with mysteries which continually elude solution by our finite minds. Our insights may help us to penetrate somewhat into their depths, but they remain ever to challenge us. They are the mysteries of our existence. The greatest is the mystery of evil, but it is flanked by the mystery of man's destiny and the mystery of creation. And ever looming behind them is the mystery of that ultimate reality, that self-sufficient, unconditioned Ground of all Being, who alone can unveil the lesser mysteries of our existence.

Reason, in the light of the God-given insights which religion claims, may seek to penetrate a little more into the darkness which besets us before and after and beneath. Such is its function, as the servant of a faith commitment to the self-giving revelation of the Ground from whom our being is derived. In doing so, because we live by faith and not by sight, it must meet the challenge of other faiths—naturalisms and atheisms especially. In such a task it will seek to demonstrate and confirm its own faith-stance. Here it must seek to show that such a stance offers a more comprehensive and coherent understanding of all human experience, giving to each such experience its valued place, and not seeking to explain it away. In so doing, reason must show that its faith-stance sheds more intelligible light upon life's dark mysteries and makes human existence itself more meaningful than do other rival claims. Rational coherence is thereby matched with the pragmatic claim to existential meaning. To this task we must turn our attention.

Scientific Knowledge and Religious Understanding— Creation and Evolution

5 Having looked at theism's understanding of God and the reality of a transcendent Presence, we must turn our attention to our world consciousness and its concomitant human self-awareness. The actuality of the world and of other persons, centering in our own self-awareness, is where the debate over religion and its insight has its testing. We have already indicated that finally our religious insights can be confirmed only by their providing a more coherent and comprehensive understanding of our world and of our human personhood and by their practical relevance to the meaning and nature of human existence.

It is just at this point that modern science has provided us with a wealth of information and also produced, as an alternative to religious belief, a naturalistic interpretation of the universe. This is in no way to disparage the natural sciences or to reject their findings. We can never turn our back upon the new understandings of man and his world which scientific investigation has opened up. Nor may we spurn the methodological approach peculiar to science. The emphasis on sense experience is basic to our life together and our life in our world. Science has made it very clear that the empirical approach to reality can yield remarkable results and increase man's control and manipulation both of his world and of his own life. This does not, however, mean that such an approach is the sole source of knowledge, and it is just here that science has made possible the emergence of its naturalistic progeny. We have already, in various ways, shown the ways in which naturalism endeavors to reduce the spiritual and moral experiences to manifestations of natural urges. Such a viewpoint has arisen because of the tremendous success of natural science in dealing with the problems of human existence. Mental and physical health, control of our natural environment, the production of food have all benefited by the results of scientific investigation and its technological applications. In consequence, science has come to be regarded as the sole way of knowledge, the norm for all understanding of the universe. It has brought forth naturalism as a by-product.

There are, of course, other ways of knowing, and it is the virtue of thinkers like A. N. Whitehead and Michael Polanyi that they have pointed to the limitations of scientific method.

The Limitations of Scientific Method

Later medievalism produced a school of thought, nominalism, which fathered modern science. The nominalists, in contrast to the hitherto dominant approach of Greek thought, were more concerned with individual things than with universal concepts. Rejecting the doctrine that the universal concept was the ultimately real, they concentrated upon the particulars and held that universals were class names arrived at by correlating the similar qualities arising in many particulars. It is not surprising that out of such a group came the first proponents of a new approach to nature—Roger Bacon, Robert Grosseteste, Jean Buridan and Nicholas Oresme. Such thinkers disparaged and rejected any preoccupation with the authority of the ancients, especially Aristotle, and called for the empirical observation of natural objects. They retained, however, the conviction that the observed structure of nature is rational in general and is basically mathematical. From Galileo onwards, the two-pronged presupposition of science has been very evident—that the realm of nature has a causative rational structure which is at basis mathematical and that this structure can be best determined by empirical observation. Thus deduction and induction, rational process and empirical observation, are alike present. Empiricism and inductive logic are matched by deductive reasoning and intuitive insight. No particular balance of these approaches can be stipulated for any specific scientific investigation. Scientific method cannot be laid out according to a rule of thumb.

Certain aspects of it, however, need to be stressed. One element in the presuppositions of natural science since its initiation has been the assumption that the structure of nature is mathematical and that this structure is empirically measurable. In part the reason for this has lain in the increasing recognition of a certain subjective and fallible element present in all sensible qualities, and hence in an effort to attain a communicable objectivity in what is observable. Color blindness and tone deafness are only extreme reminders that the sensible qualities of taste, smell, color, sound and touch are variable. But measurements are, to a much higher degree, less subject to the physiological and psychological variabilities of the observer. Hence fundamentally all science has a mathematical base, and exact science increasingly seeks for such a base, often at the cost of reducing the sciences of life and mind to the level of physics, chemistry, and statistics. It would be true to say that the physical sciences offer the true point of reference for all natural science and that scientific method must regard these as its ideal norm.

In consequence of this, the scientist has been concerned to find some intelligible model which enables him to understand his world and which is subject to mathematical formulation. In the earlier and classical period of natural science, the era of Newton and his successors, such models were sought at the geometrical level, and mechanical causation was regarded as the key. The natural universe was pictured as a mechanical structure in which solid billiard-ball-like atoms, in motion and in evermore complex structural patterns, behaved in a purely mechanical fashion in an absolute framework of space and time. The idea of mechanical causation was central. The basis of this idea undoubtedly lay in the human experience of personal causation through mental and bodily activity. Indeed, this personal model is found in the primitive philosophy of animism and, in a highly developed form, in Aristotle's philosophy. Natural science, however, denuded such an idea of any association with teleology, motivation towards goals, final causation. Efficient causation replaced final or teleological causation, and the attempt was made to disassociate such causation from any subjective or personal aspects. The model for the world became lumps of matter related to one another in a pattern of mechanical causation. Here the analytical dimension of reason seemed to rule supreme. Familiar and understood mechanical phenomena provided models for the unfamiliar and incomprehensible. The atoms and molecules in a gas were envisaged on the model of billiard balls on collision course. Light and radiation were pictured in the model of waves on the sea. The solar planetary system became a model for the atom with its nucleus and orbiting electrons. Such models were tested by means of experimental apparatus based on them, and once they were verified, they became the basis for rational predictions and developments and also for further experimental investigation.

As science progressed, the Newtonian mechanistic picture was challenged in various ways. At the turn of this century, the ideas of absolute space and absolute time were challenged and gave place to the relativistic picture of Albert Einstein. Space and time measurements were shown to be relative to the particular observer. Absolute matter could no longer be maintained, as the atom itself was found to be no longer solid, as a mysterious world of sub-atomic particles was disclosed to shake man's confidence in the billiard-ball atom and molecule, as radiation was shown to possess a corpuscular as well as a wave form, as a similar duality was discovered in so-called material particles, and as the transformation of matter into radiation and vice versa became an established fact. Finally, absolute causation was replaced by behavior which could only be expressed statistically or in terms of probability.

It has become increasingly evident that scientific models must not be taken literally. This was possible when the models were picturable. Even then nature was pictured in a very abstract way. The emphasis on measurement led to a view of the world in which the latter was stripped even of all those sense qualities that make it so rich and meaningful. We were left, and we still are, at the scientific level, with an abstract world from which color and sound, beauty and music, scents and warmth disappear. Of such a world, A. N. Whitehead wrote: "The bodies are perceived as with qualities which in reality do not belong to them, qualities which in fact are purely the offspring of the mind. Thus nature gets credit which should in truth be reserved for ourselves: the rose for its scent; the nightingale for his song; and the sun for his radiance. The poets are entirely mistaken. They should address their lyrics to themselves, and should turn them into odes of self-congratulation on the excellence of the human mind. Nature is a dull affair, soundless, scentless, colorless; merely the hurrying of material, endlessly, meaninglessly" (A. N. Whitehead, *Science and the Modern World*, Cambridge: The University Press, 1932, pp. 134f.).

Such a view still underlies the scientific viewpoint, but it no longer takes its models literally, for they have now become increasingly mathematical. The analytical reason is still in control, and the process of abstraction has gone on until modern physics and chemistry are concerned with abstract mathematical equations. The elements of measurable objectivity and communication are retained, however, and scientists still concern themselves with measurable observables. The theory of relativity has retained communication at the center of the scientists' world by relating the various variable frames of measurement through the invariable nature of the speed of light, the radiation by which communications can take place.

A. N. Whitehead accuses scientific methodology, with its analytical procedures, of 'the fallacy of misplaced concreteness'. He defines this fallacy as accepting as real what has been abstracted from reality as an object of thought. If we separate an entity from its environment and then describe it in its abstract condition, we are not describing it at all in its concrete actuality. In science, we are creating a symbolic image which will fit into our mathematical pattern. The scientific approach thus manifests 'the fallacy of simple location'. It abstracts from the rich interrelationships and wholeness of the world of immediate awareness an array of lumps of matter, separated in space and moving in time. This isolation does violence, Whitehead contends, to the organic unity of our world. It requires mechanical causation or, more abstractly, mathematical relationships to provide the cement between what we have artificially separated in space and time.

This process of abstraction becomes much more evident today when we have moved from mechanical models to those drawn from pure mathematical analyses. Despite attempts to popularize what science is saying in the complex mathematical language of relativity theory and quantum physics, all that can be offered is at best a skeleton outline of that rich world which we immediately experience. This outline has been likened to a flat map from which the rich contours and reliefs of actuality have been removed.

Yet it does, to some degree, correspond to reality. We must in no way disparage the success and significance of science at its own level.

For even in the choosing of models intuitive insight comes into play, and what we have called earlier the synthetic or holistic dimension of reason begins to function. The great advances in science have come, not just by a pedestrian combination, in differing proportions, of empirical observation and analytical reasoning, but rather by an *intuitive hunch* in which much of the preceding structure of theory and models has been swept away. In our century we have seen this happen with the theory of relativity, the quantum theory, and the application of mathematical group theory to physical analysis. The experimental observation of the invariable nature of the speed of light by Michelson and Morley called forth many attempts, such as those of Lorentz and Fitzgerald, to explain this invariability within the accepted structure. It was Einstein who, with intuitive insight, introduced his revolutionary ideas and, borrowing from the pure mathematical theories of tensor analysis and Riemannian geometry, suggested a radical new approach which swept away much of the old structure. It was the intuitive insights of men like de Broglie, Sommerfeld, Bohr, Born, and Heisenberg which followed up the experimental investigations of Planck on radiation and Rutherford on the atom and provided a revolutionary approach to atomic structure. Such insights have transformed our view of the universe. To them we must add the intuitive hunch of Dirac and Eddington whereby the relativistic viewpoint was combined with the new quantum theory by utilizing the abstract mathematical theory of groups. The latter had no relationship to such physical phenomena but arose originally in the geometrical analysis of Kümmer's quartic surface! Incidentally, in biology, it was the intuitive hunch of Darwin which applied the sociological investigations of Malthus to nature and exposed some of the mechanism of evolution. The interesting point is that the mathematical structures were already available and the empirical observations challenging the older scientific theories were at hand, but it waited for the intuitive insight to bring them together.

Various factors may be discerned in this intuitive insight. One is the recognition of the utility of Occam's razor, that it is impractical to multiply unobservable entities in order to retain a challenged theoretical structure. Another is an aesthetic element, very evident in attempts to delineate the structure of the complex carbon compounds such as the ring-compounds, but also evident in the recognition of simplicity and harmonious order in certain mathematical formulations. But, finally, the intuitive insights would seem to suggest that there is in science a synthetic as well as an analytic approach to reality, and that the intuitive grasping of a whole is often more significant than the mere analysis of the parts. Polanyi has made us very aware of what he has called the 'tacit dimension' of knowing. He has argued that the scientist is tacitly aware of a patterned wholeness before he begins his investigation and that science involves a personal commitment, a heuristic passion, which is bound up with such awareness. A scientific search arises out of an intimation of the unknown, a tacit awareness that awakens a passionate commitment to scientific quest. Polanyi describes this as a 'plunging faculty'. He suggests that we are "guided by our power for seeing the presence of some hidden comprehensive entity behind yet incomprehensible clues pointing increasingly towards this yet unknown entity" (M. Polanyi, Ms. *Faith and Reason*, p. 5). Thus the forms of the analytical reason, inductive and deductive, "operate only as the intellectual roots of man's tacit powers reaching toward the hidden meaning of things" (*ibid.*, p. 5). We may see, behind the preoccupation of science with the analytical dimension of reason, the synthetic dimension within which intuitive insight arises.

In this intuitive insight, disparate and widely distributed data are integrated into a new and often revolutionary pattern. The intuition and the experimentation are often mutually stimulating, and what we find is of one piece with the emphasis on Gestalt psychology in our normal process of perception. Often this grasping of the whole may precede the discovery of much experimental data and may lead to new forms of experimentation in which its insights are confirmed. One important aspect of scientific advance is the way in which such insights bring about new and unanticipated disclosures of the structure of the natural order.

This suggests that the models which form the basic elements of scientific theories are molded to natural reality. The error is when the natural order is so identified with the model that the analogical nature of the model is ignored. Because it is an analogy, all aspects of the model are not necessarily applicable to the structure of nature. The more embracing the analogy and more prolific the new avenues of natural knowledge it opens, the closer it is to the structure of nature that we are seeking to understand. Thus correspondingly the intuitive insight or tacit awareness in which the particular model is grounded is closer to reality, some aspect of whose wholeness it is grasping. There is a 'given' to which the scientist is responding, but the true scientist is also aware of how much mystery remains and eludes his grasp. The deeper he penetrates into nature, the more fresh problems arise.

Because science is employing models, often some aspects of the model produce an illusive idea about nature itself. Thus the mechanical models, so favored by classical science, led to the accepted view of nature being dominated by causal determinism. Too close an identification of the model with the structure of nature produced a materialistic dogmatism which robbed man of his freedom and drove God out of his world. Such ideas have persisted in contemporary naturalism where life and mind are reduced to the level of manifestations of natural forces and energies. It is, of course, equally dangerous to emphasize too much the contemporary emphasis on laws as statistical averages and upon the acausal and 'probability' aspects of quantum physics. If this is stressed too much, religious faith stands to lose as much in a world dominated by chance as it does in one dominated by determinism. That there is a logos, a rational structure, in the deeps of nature is still a deep seated and tacit assumption by the true scientist.

Science, as Whitehead pointed out, has, however, almost ignored the holistic or synthetic dimension of knowing. Analysis has become dominant with the conviction that the natural order can be completely understood by an analysis of its parts and that there is nothing trans-empirical. Polanyi has differentiated the two ways of knowing as an intuitive grasping of wholes and a concentration on the various constituent parts in a whole. He has reminded us that as we concentrate on the one way of knowing, the other fades into the background. Thus the synthetic type of awareness of a whole tends to push into the background our awareness of the particular elements in that whole. On the other hand, the analytic type of awareness concentrates on the particular elements and loses sight of the whole of which they are constituents and to which they point as clues. It is of the essence of the rationalistic and thus of the scientific method that it tends to be analytic, to explain the whole by building it up out of its constituents. And this is true, despite the fact that its greatest advances have arisen through an intuitive hunch, a grasping of some *Gestalt*, some patterned whole in nature. In consequence of this emphasis, science tends to be weighted in a naturalistic direction. Consequently we have an increasing preoccupation with biophysics, bio-chemistry, and various behavioristic forms of psychology.

Nature as a Developing Process of Wholes and the Naturalistic Challenge

We turn now to examine the world-structure which science presents to us. As we have seen, at best this is a map from which the contours and relief perspective are omitted. We need always to remember that science is concerned only with what is empirically observable. The latter is given a broad definition in the sense that science does speak about entities, such as some sub-atomic particles, which are only theoretically observable, but certainly there is excluded from its concern qua science any possible referents to which the words 'life', 'mind', 'soul', 'spirit', 'God', etc. apply. If it uses the words 'life' and 'mind' they are solely descriptive of certain kinds of observable behavior and can have no reference to any transempirical entity.

The scientific description of the process by which man appeared on this planet sees an ascent from the stage of inanimate structures through that of animate beings with various degrees of consciousness to that of self-conscious man. The whole universe is pictured as beginning with a big explosion of energy from which, in a small period of time, all the sub-atomic particles and the atomic structures were soon formed and out of which whirling masses the galaxies separated with their constituent stellar masses and with maybe planetary satellites around many of the latter. On the planet called earth, formed in some way from the stellar material of our sun, a process went on in which a gaseous and molten mass slowly cooled to produce, by chemical combinations, the liquid, gaseous and solid structures which make up our space ship (for this is what it is). As the air attained its present state and moisture accumulated in it and on the ground, chemical changes were going on as increasing molecular complexity was attained. The presence of the element carbon, together with the gases hydrogen and oxygen, made possible this development of complex molecular structures without which life, as we know it, would be impossible.

The complex carbon compounds ultimately became sufficiently

complex for rudimentary living things to appear, maybe in the depths of the primordial ocean and under the impact of the intense electrical storms which were of frequent occurrence. Even now, scientists can identify the grey and shadowy zone between the living and the non-living. The presence of viruses is an instance of this.

Science, because even matter and radiation are forms of energy, tends to regard energy as the basic stuff. Energy is difficult to define except as something dynamic, something that acts. Whatever it may be in its essential form, the scientist knows it empirically in its basic structures as matter or radiation, each transformable into the other under certain conditions. 'Energy' is thus an abstraction which is never known except in concrete forms, from electrons, protons, neutrons, photons or quanta of radiation, through atoms, molecules, viruses, animal organic structures to human bodies. Nature manifests the capacity of energy for getting knotted up into more complex physical wholes.

This quality of wholeness is evident at the inorganic level. Even the once simple atom is now recognized as a highly complex pattern of energy with components like electrons, protons, neutrons, mesons and an increasing number of sub-atomic particles such as quarks. What we see in the inorganic becomes more evident when we move to viruses, the unicellular organisms like amoeba with which life began, and the increasingly complex structures which make up the animal order. Such wholes have a unity in activity and a pattern of relationships between their constituent parts such that new qualities become evident which those parts do not manifest separately. It has been pointed out that the hardness of diamonds, the conductive properties of copper, and the magnetic properties of iron result from the way in which the basic atoms and molecules are ordered and interrelated.

At the frontier between the inorganic and the organic we find the double helix structure of the DNA molecule which is the organizing center for organisms. Once such genetic structures were formed and housed in a certain chemical habitat, there was a fundamental difference in the new wholeness which appeared. There was that new quality which we call 'life', and it was associated with a new form of patterned relationship between the constituent parts. We can see this when we compare and contrast inanimate structures like crystals with dynamic organic structures like tadpole eggs. Crystals and polymers, like modern synthetic fibers, grow by external additions. The key to growth is external aggregation. On the other hand, organisms grow by internal differentiation. Suitable material from the environment is ingested and then, by chemical processes, broken down to develop the structure of the organism from within. Directed by enzyme messengers from the genetic nuclei of the cells, the organism both multiplies its cells and also differentiates their specific functions. Here the key to growth is internal differentiation.

There is also an integrative unity in organisms. They are differentiated into many parts and organs, and yet these function in the service of the whole. Their wholeness became increasingly centralized as the developmental process of nature continued on this planet. Outwardly this centralized complexity was manifested in individuality and thus its advent marked the beginning of selfhood. Physiologically the wholes became increasingly centralized as the nervous system and the sense organs were centralized in a developing cerebrum. Brain development is a significant aspect of growing selfhood in the evolutionary process. Psychically such developments were associated with a movement from sentience or rudimentary feeling to consciousness and then self-consciousness. It has been pointed out that the increasing complexity of living wholes at the level of the animals and the primates is associated with the brain and the centralized nervous system. This increasing consciousness was matched by new ways of responding to the environment.

This indicates another differentiating characteristic of living wholes—their relative independence of the environment with accompanying self motion. Inanimate groupings of energy behave mechanically. They have to be moved by external forces and are incapable of self motion. Magnetic and electric fields, additions of energy from without and accompanying excitation alone make movement possible. At the physicochemical level, the interaction between the constituent entities is observable in mechanistic and mathematical terms. Once 'life' makes itself evident, we find a capacity for self movement in the most rudimentary living beings, even to some degree in plants. The pattern or organization of the living whole is seen, not only in its differentiation of specific organs, but also in the presence of inborn impulses or instincts which determine the functions that such organs serve. In the process of evolution, organisms have survived by virtue of the development of such organs with their accompanying instinctual functions.

At the lower levels of living things, such responsive behavior is rigidly mechanical, innate and determined from within. Such beginnings of self motion develop with the appearance of consciousness, however, and as living wholes move up the scale of complexity, there is increasing ability to adapt itself to its environment. There is a growing capacity to learn by experience, to modify instinctual urges, and to adapt the organism by such learnt ways to a different environment. Feeling moves into consciousness. Learning and animal memory appear and betoken what, at the human level, we call 'mind'. The details of actions can be modified to meet a specific situation. Finally, with self-conscious man we have not merely a capacity to learn by experience and adapt the self to the environment, but a capacity to adapt the environment to oneself. With thought came the ability to control the environment and change it for one's own purposes.

What science discloses is thus a hierarchy of wholes. The lowest or inanimate level manifests comparative simplicity when examined from the level of highly developed mammalian structures. However, despite the arguments of naturalists, we cannot deny that the appearance of behavior describable as 'life', 'mind' or consciousness, self-conscious mind or 'spirit' points to an ascending scale of wholes which manifest new ways of adaptation to environment and finally of controlling that environment in their own interests with the appearance of man and his cultural activity.

Scientific reductionism tends to ignore this hierarchy of levels, and, in its form of naturalism, presents a challenge to any who believe that 'life', 'mind' and 'spirit' represent 'something more' than mere physics and chemistry. We have already pointed out that knowledge does not begin with an examination of the parts from which we infer the whole. Rather, tacit knowledge of the whole sets us out on the scientific quest. In the latter we focus our attention on the parts, but comprehension requires us to return to the whole. The error of naturalism and its reductionism is just this exclusive concentration on the parts. When biology adopts the analytical approach of the physical sciences, it is unable to deal adequately with living wholes at any of the higher levels. For it can take Humpty-Dumpty to pieces, but it has no way of dealing with the quality which makes Humpty-Dumpty more than a mere aggregation of parts. Indeed, it is unable to assemble such parts and produce Humpty-Dumpty. It cannot put Humpty-Dumpty together again! E. W. Sinnott has reminded us that "a living thing is not a collection of parts and traits but an *organized system*, well called an *organism* "(E. W. Sinnott, *The Bridge of Life: From Matter to Spirit*, New York: Simon and Schuster, 1966, p. 65). The naturalist or reductionist ignores such a warning. He needs to remember that living things manifest a biological type of organization which cannot be reduced to the level of physics and chemistry and satisfactorily explained. 'Life' is physics and chemistry and 'something more'! So too with 'mind' and 'spirit'. Biochemistry and biophysics are necessary for the understanding of the whole, yet they do not give a full comprehension of the organism, for they cannot disclose the nature of the organizing principle of the whole.

The tendency ever since Descartes to use the machine model for living things has been reinforced by the invention of computers and of devices fitted with homing devices such as the destructive rockets used in modern air warfare. Such a naturalistic approach often forgets that machines are human artifacts and that to understand them we need more than knowledge of the physics and chemistry of their parts. They are aggregates humanly organized and manifesting human intention. We need to know the operational principles underlying their structure and the purpose which they are to serve in order to understand them. Indeed, our description of a machine at the physical level always directly or indirectly includes the personal aspect of purpose, the intention behind the construction. Even the machine has a higher level of organization than the mere physical aggregation of its parts. The operation of this organizing principle depends, of course, upon the physicochemical laws which govern the parts. It is conditioned by them for successful operation, but it is not explained by them.

The living organism is not an artifact, but the machine does offer an analogy by which to understand the structural pattern of such an organic whole. It is significant that the biologist, however much he may be committed to a naturalistic and reductionist viewpoint, cannot avoid the use of terms like 'aim', 'purpose', 'adaptation', 'regulation' which properly belong to our personal experience. However much he may seek to remove the subjective and personal reference and use such terms in the setting of physicochemical explanation, he is implying an organization in living things which has some teleogical dimension and which transcends the physicochemical order. It is significant that we human beings have a sense of 'kinship' with living things as if we feel in them an organizing principle near to our sense of purposive wholeness. It is more true of animals than of machines that our understanding of them requires more than a knowledge of their physics and chemistry. If machines are irreducible to physics and chemistry,the more should it be impossible for organic beings to be so reduced. As Polanyi has remarked: "the recognition of organismic processes no longer bears the burden of standing alone as evidence for the irreducibility of living things" (M. Polanyi, *Knowing and Being*, Chicago: University of Chicago Press, 1969, p. 232).

This indicates that the physicochemical laws which govern the parts of an organism can never account for the organizing principle of the higher whole. As Polanyi puts it, the higher entity "is logically unspecifiable in terms of its particulars" (M. Polanyi, *The Study of Man*, Chicago: University of Chicago Press, Phoenix Books, 1963, p. 45), and its operations are not explicable in terms of the laws that apply to those particulars (cf. M. Polanyi, *Tacit Knowledge*, New York: Anchor Books, 1966, pp. 38ff.). Polanyi suggests the term 'the principle of marginal control' for the relation of the organizing principle to the parts which it employs. The laws of the lower levels to which the parts belong—for example the physicochemical laws which hold for the parts of a machine or for the constituents of a living whole—leave unspecified the boundary conditions within which they are to operate. These boundary conditions are set by the organizing principle of the higher level. The lower level leaves possibilities for operation within conditions fixed by the organizing principle of the higher. Applying this to living things, in the whole range of hierarchical levels, he writes:

> The vegetative system, sustaining life at rest, leaves open the possibilities of bodily movements by means of muscular action, and the principles of muscular action leave open their integration into innate patterns of behavior. Such patterns leave open, once more, their shaping by intelligence, the working of which offers, in its turn, wide-

ranging possibilities for the exercise of still higher principles in those of us who possess them (*ibid.*, p. 41).

We are left with a hierarchy of levels stretching up from the physicochemical level through the various organizations that we call living things to the level of man himself, of personal being. In every case, the principles of the lower levels operate under the control of the principles of the higher levels which set the boundaries within which the former are to operate. No level can control its own boundary conditions, which are set by the higher level. This would suggest that we need a concept of emergence in order to understand the evolutionary process. Questions appropriate to a higher level cannot be answered at a lower level. So we have to examine how the new organizing principles, labelled 'life', 'mind', 'spirit', appear in the natural process.

Evolution and Emergence

So far as the mechanism of biological evolution is concerned, the scientific consensus supports the Neo-Darwinian position. On this view, the major changes in the evolutionary process came as the result of the interaction of environmental selectiveness and small random mutations in the genetic structures, the DNA molecules of the organisms. Under certain conditions, such small random mutations could aggregate into a major change of species. Thus the model first devised by Darwin is still in the ascendant, and the expressions 'survival of the fittest' and 'natural selection' are still significant. Darwin's small chance variations have been replaced by small random mutations, and the mechanism has been clearly defined by the recognition of the significant part played by the genetic structures. Neo-Darwinians emphasize the time factor and contend that the long duration of the evolutionary process is sufficient to account for the large-scale transformations on the basis of random small mutations. R. A. Fisher has sought to show, on statistical grounds, that natural selection combined with a slow rate of such mutation is sufficient to account for the origin of species (*vide* R. A. Fisher, *The Genetical Theory of Natural Selection*, Oxford: Oxford University Press, 1930).

Dobzhansky, the dean of American biologists, has somewhat modified the model by suggesting the occasional occurrence of larger mutations. He calls these 'quantum mutations' and suggests that in these, many traits are changed together with mutual reinforcement. He finds such a quantum mutation in the emergence of man in which many new characteristics—upright stance, tools, symbolic language, change in food habits, relaxation of male aggressiveness, monogamous family—most likely came together with a mutuality that produced a novel situation. He can describe such quantum mutations as rare occurrences and suggests that they are unlikely to involve changes of one trait at a time. He remains, however, a committed Neo-Darwinian, and to this position there is no organized opposition. Certain biologists, like Dalcq, Vandel, and others, hold that the major developments in the process occurred through 'onto-mutations' in which the whole organismic structure was involved and not just the genetic molecules. Such thinkers would confine the Neo-Darwinian model to changes *within* a species. Generally, however, the latter model provides the orthodox biological viewpoint for understanding the evolutionary process.

This theory has, ever since the time of T. H. Huxley, been a valuable asset in the naturalistic challenge. For it suggests that the process is a continuous one in which the physicochemical structures of the genetic material are the sole determining factors. It is simply a matter of energy, purely physical in nature, taking on new complexities. Furthermore, it does so accidentally. The changes are random, and statistical mathematics would support the case that, given the long span of millions of years, such changes could accumulate to produce the present condition of nature, including, of course, man.

Such a challenge can be met at three points. The first would be the argument already made that 'life', 'mind', 'spirit' involve 'something more' than mere physicochemical structures of energy, however complex. The second would be that science defines energy in too narrow a way by confining it to its measurable and physical dimensions. Lloyd Morgan and C. D. Broad, among others, have introduced the word 'emergence' to describe the way that the 'something more' appears in the process. C. D. Broad expresses this as the actualization in a vital whole of properties latent in the physicochemical constituents. This actualization becomes possible because of new relations into which these constituents enter in the organism. Emergence means, therefore, that what is potential in energy becomes actual when certain levels of organization or structural relationship are attained.

On this basis, we find Teilhard de Chardin postulating two dimensions for energy, a tangential one responsible for physical proliferation and a radial one responsible for the internal development towards mind and spirit. Nature has a 'within' as well as a 'without'. With the inner side, science qua science is powerless to deal, and yet this has carried the secret of the whole process. To quote Teilhard:

> Beneath the "tangential" we find the "radial." The impetus of the world, glimpsed in the great drive of consciousness, can only have its ultimate source in some *inner* principle, which alone could explain its irreversible advance towards higher psychisms" (Teilhard de Chardin, *The Phenomenon of Man*, trans. Bernard Wall, New York: Harper & Bros., 1959, p. 149).

Thus the emergence of 'life' results from an explosion of "internal energy" which lifts the process out of the physicochemical level to the organic level and provides a new organizing principle. Teilhard likens it to a change of state, so familiar in physical science, when a liquid becomes gaseous, for example.

This brings us to the third point of rebuttal—the demonstration of purposive or teleogical aspects in the natural process. There is, at the level of the individual organisms, a pattern of organization which is reflected in the definite way in which the organism moves ahead until the end of the whole is attained. Instinctual drive presents the same characteristics as consciousness and self-consciousness do in the responsiveness of higher levels of living wholes to the environment. In these higher beings, including man, the means have changed but, so long as the end is attained, we might describe the behavior at all levels as 'purposive'. Indeed, as E. S. Russell has pointed out: "we recognize the fact that organic activities as manifested by organized unities such as cells and organisms, show characteristics, especially in their directiveness, persistency and adaptability which are shown also in instinctive and intelligent behavior of ourselves and other animals" (E. S. Russell, *The Directiveness of Organic Activities*, Cambridge: Cambridge University Press, 1945, p. 179). A pattern seems to regulate growth and to control behavior by setting goals for the organism to attain. Once more we find evidence for the presence of the organizing principle to which we referred earlier. We can understand the comment of E. W. Sinnott: "In behavior, protoplasmic purpose grows to instinct, and with dawning consciousness this leads to thought and the higher elements of mind" (E. W. Sinnott, *Matter, Mind and Man*, New York: Harper & Bros., 1957, pp. 43f.).

When we turn from the individual organism to the whole process with its hierarchy of levels, we seem to find evidence again of a purposive drive, a nisus towards higher forms. There are those who accept the mechanism postulated by Neo-Darwinism and yet can speak of creativity in the process or of a mysterious coordination of the micromutations. Polanyi and Dobzhansky are examples, as also Teilhard. Indeed, our attack is not on Neo-Darwinism as a viable model, but on those who use it as a basis for their naturalism. Even so ardent an advocate of the Neo-Darwinian model as Sir Julian Huxley can write: "The primacy of human personality has been . . . a *postulate* both of Christianity and liberal democracy, but it is a *fact* of evolution. By whatever objective standards we choose to take, properly developed human personalities are the highest products of evolution" (J. S. Huxley, *Evolution in Action*, New York: Harper & Bros., 1953). Such an evaluation implies that life and man are more than mere accidents in a chancy process. All through the process we have evidence of emergent qualities which are unpredictable in terms of what has preceded them. But they do not appear as the result of accident or as random happenings. Rather they have marked the major steps in the progressive movement of the natural order. The emergence of living wholes, of conscious beings, of self-conscious persons—these are creative advances. As W. H. Thorpe writes:

> I think we are perfectly justified in calling these events "miracles," divesting the term of its personal associations . . . . I suggest that they may be regarded as miracles in the sense that they appear to be essentially unforeseeable, while at the same time exhibiting overall consistency—the kind of general consistency that the evolutionary process itself had displayed. (W. H. Thorpe, *Biology and the Nature of Man*, London: Oxford University Press, 1962, p. 18).

It is this consistency in the hierarchy of levels leading to the emergence of man which points to something more than the naturalist would have us discern, some inner drive, some purposive nisus. So we are ready to look at the theistic understanding of the world-structure which science provides.

Absolute Creation and Its Religious Alternatives

The scientific world-structure and its picture of nature as a developing process now have to be understood within a theistic setting. In so doing, we have to look at other religious options, the naturalistic option having already been considered. The religious views generally fall into two groups—a monistic group and a dualistic group—and these correspond to two philosophical formulations of the relationship of the deity to the world.

Let us first of all make clear what we mean by 'to create'. Its normal meaning is 'to bring into being'. Now this may signify either 'to originate absolutely' or merely 'to shape a certain form from pre-existing material'. It is the latter meaning which expresses the relation of the deity to the world in both the groups just mentioned.

The monistic group includes both pantheistic and panentheistic systems. In its pantheistic form the idea of creation is absent. God is the sole reality and that reality is identified with the world. It is in the panentheistic form that the idea of creation appears, though in a very vague likeness at times. In panentheism, the world is derived from the deity's own being, either by a necessary process in the deity or by a voluntaristic and intentional act on the part of the deity.

In the first type of panentheism, the world emanates from God as a necessary result of the super-abundance of the divine essence. This is specifically expressed in Neo-Platonism. The world is an efflux of God, a "byplay of contemplation," a necessary development of the deity, whose life passes into human souls and nature and returns from them again. Such emanation, since it is involuntary, can hardly be described as 'creation'. We should note, however, that, as with all forms of panentheism, there is no break in the transition from the Source of all being to its consequent, the world.

The second type of panentheism is specifically foreshadowed in Hegel's form of absolute idealism. Here the necessity in the divine being is not a natural one as in Neo-Platonism, but a logical one. The very rational nature of the Absolute Spirit, who again is the *sole* reality, leads it to seek self-realization in the process of nature and history. Thus the world is a rational expression of the Absolute. It is God spelling himself out logically in time. History and nature manifest the pattern of God's logical dialectic as they move through theses, antitheses and syntheses. God expresses himself subjectively in persons and objectively in social structures and natural processes. Thus human beings and all other finite actualities have only adjectival existence. They are temporary manifestations of deity, and any seeming freedom is simply the expression of the logical movement of the Absolute. We might refer to the world as a creation but it is a logical creation existing in God's own being and fulfilling his rational needs and intentions.

Later systems of thought have been influenced by Hegel's approach but express the concept of creation much more clearly—still, of course, creation out of the divine substance! We may think of the philosophies of Royce, Hocking, Hartshorne and Tillich, all of whom lay claim to expressing the Christian faith, though certainly not in the form of classical theism. So we turn to the more specific expressions of the second type of panentheism, in which God voluntarily forms the world 'out of his own stuff'. The world results from an act of the divine will as an expression of a divine intention. It is thus created, but created out of the divine substance. Those who hold this view imply that the world is necessary for God, and that, in producing it out of his own being, he is voluntarily expressing a necessity of his own nature. Such systems evidently retain a continuity between the divine being and the world. They give little or no scope for human freedom. It is difficult to associate real freedom with beings who are, in their essence, finite manifestations, 'fragments', of the divine substance. Sin tends to be associated with finitude, negative deficiency rather than positive rebellion. It is deprivation rather than depravity. Freedom easily degenerates into determinism. The activities of such beings tend to become expressions of the divine will. By blending the Being of God with beings who issue from him, even though it be by an act of his will, such thought has a further difficulty. It has to explain how such a spiritual emanation can have the appearance of a material and spatially extended universe. Indeed, in all forms of panentheism, creation is really emanation, involuntary or voluntary.

The alternative to this monistic stance is the dualistic one. This meets the last stated difficulty by frankly propounding an eternal dualism of God and the pre-existent stuff out of which he shapes the world. We find this in Plato's *Timaeus* where the deity becomes a demi-urge dealing with an opposing inertia (ἀνάγκη) in the nature of things which is independent of the divine mind. Elsewhere Plato speaks of the *chora* (χώρα), the receptacle, or not-being, *meon*. Aristotle introduces matter (ὕλη). Many early mythologies speak of a primordial chaos which the deity shaped into order. God is a constructor rather than a creator, that is to say, than an absolute creator. The Christian Church had soon to struggle with dualism in combating the Gnostics. Irenaeus became a strong opponent of these, and later Augustine took up cudgels against the dualism of the Manicheans, according to whom God created the world out of material which is inherently evil.

This brings us to the theistic position and its doctrine of 'creation out of nothing', *ex nihilo*. It stands as does the Christian faith of which it is a dechristianized expression, between panentheism and dualism, seeking to fall into the pits of neither. It was first explicitly and fully expressed by Irenaeus, whose statement is worth quoting: "To attribute the substance of created things to the power and will of Him who is God of all, is worthy of both credit and acceptance. It is also agreeable to reason, and there may well be said, regarding such a belief, that 'the things which are impossible with men are possible with God.' While men indeed cannot make anything out of nothing, but only out of matter already existing, yet God is at this point preeminently superior to men, that He Himself called into being the substance of His creation, when previously it had no existence" (*Adv. Haer.* II, x. 3 and 4). For theism there is not independent material, no part or element of being which does not owe its existence to its Creator. All that has being depends upon the will of God. The created world exists by the intention and free decision of the Creator. God is under no necessity to create, and so he is totally responsible for his world. Thereby the 'Scylla and Charybdis' of dualism and panentheism are both avoided. Furthermore, as against panentheistic emanationism, theism preserves the relative independence and freedom of finite beings.

Theism maintains the relative independence of such created beings while, at the same time, emphasizing the dependence of all things on God. It does so by envisaging the divine activity in the form of will and by postulating, for finite spirits, a moral freedom and responsibility which reflect, in small measure, the nature of the deity. Every creature is completely dependent on God and yet enjoys its 'being-for-selfness' at its own level of being. This can be because they are posited, called into being by his free creative decision, and not derived from his substance.

James Ward draws an analogy for creation from the creative genius of a writer or an artist, and this kind of analogy needs to be pursued, even though it is at best faint and distant. A creative novelist can so deal with his plot that the characters which he creates suddenly come alive, achieve individuality, and begin to act within the artist's mind. Such novelists will tell us that the story begins to tell itself. Even their own intentions and plans for the story may have to be changed as these characters begin to limit their freedom as the writer. The characters which have been created may refuse to fit into the preconceived plot. They seem to assert their individuality and demand that the development of the story change its course. They are wholly dependent upon the artist who has created them, and yet they have attained a certain objectivity which gives them a relative independence as the novel develops.

This analogy must not be pressed too far, for human genius requires a medium in which to express itself, the written page or the artist's canvas. On the other hand, the creative will of God needs no such medium. Again, the artistic work, once committed to writing and published or expressed on the canvas and displayed to the public, attains an objectivity which almost releases it from its author. On the other hand, the object of the divine will must always remain in living relationship to and constant dependence upon God. Further, we must not think of ourselves literally as characters in a story which God is telling either for his own amusement or for his own self-expression. The latter idea would bring us very near Hegel. The analogy can, indeed, be used in an adverse way, when we remember the tragedy and heartbreak and suffering in our human existence. It has been so used by thinkers like Bertrand Russell to paint a picture of a cruel and malicious deity who derives ironic pleasure from the drama of human existence (*vide* B. Russell, *A Free Man's Worship*).

It is clear that the idea of absolute creation must at the same time allow for relative dependence on the part of the creature and, in the case of man, the reality of freedom. The latter is certainly not really possible with panentheism, least of all in its form of absolute idealism or neoplatonic emanationism. It is, of course, impossible in the case of pantheism. It would be true to say that where, in such systems, some bowing acknowledgement of freedom is made, it usually means, as Leonard Hodgson suggests, that "what we think to be acts of our free choice, chosen from among other possibilities in a world of genuine contingencies, are really events predetermined by God who can see, as we cannot, how luminously intelligible they are in their place in the pattern of the whole" (L. Hodgson, *For Faith and Freedom*, New York: Charles Scribner's Sons, 1956, p. 143). Our experience of contingency and freedom is an illusion, not real. We must defer to the next chapter our further discussion of human freedom. Here, it is sufficient to note that the analogy just used does indicate that the concept of absolute creation does leave room for relative independence and freedom on the part of the creatures. The break in continuity between the beings and their Ground, which the *ex nihilo* introduces, may be irrational, but it confirms man's experience of the reality of his freedom and yet assures the utter dependence of the creation upon the will of the Creator.

Continuous Creation, Time and Process

One immediately vexing issue with which we have not dealt is the problem of a beginning of creation and of the place of time in the life of God. Once more, we must shelve until later a full discussion of the nature of the divine eternity. Here it will suffice to affirm that if God has any relation to human life, time must to that extent enter into his consciousness. But God cannot be in time, with its before and after, as we experience it. He cannot have the same relation as we to our time nor can he be subject to it as we are. His eternity is not just temporal everlastingness, but equally it is not timeless being.

This issue does affect the way in which creation is related to the time process. Obviously, since absolute creation has its source in the divine will, the creation of a process in time has a real place in the life of God. If that creation was itself in time, then God would appear to be in time. Augustine, it may be remembered, told the story of the man who replied to the question: "What was God doing before creation?"

that he was making a hell for the inquisitive. (*Confessions* xi, 12).
Actually, prior to Augustine, Origen has gone further and suggested
that creation was an eternal activity of God. God is the creator of a
realm of spirits from eternity so that creation is not an act of God but
rather a continuing activity of God. Then our universe is but one
instance of such activity. Creation qua creation is a manifestation of
that self-activity which is God's life, and other universes than ours may
be the product of that activity. There is the profound affirmation in the
Theologia Germanica that it is the property of Will to will something
and that, in order for it to have work to do, it must have creatures
(chapter 51).

Certainly we must not think of creation as an act but rather as a
continuing activity and, as such, as an activity the results of which are
meaningful in God's life. This might suggest that there is a temporal
dimension in God's eternity. We need not accept the views propounded by absolute idealists in the Hegelian succession or process
thinkers in the tradition of A. N. Whitehead and Charles Hartshorne
in order to incorporate this in a theistic understanding of God. If we
regard God as personal and as will, then he is active and self-express-
ive. We may take note of Origen's comment that "it is at once impious
and absurd to say that the nature of God is inactive and immovable, as
to suppose that goodness at one time did no good . . ." (*De Principiis*,
iii, 5.3, Crombie's translation). Furthermore, if the mark of our finite
personality is to be creative, we might expect this still more of God.
Creation is no passing and insignificant aspect of God's life. It does
make a difference whether he creates or does not create. It might even
seem that God would cease to be personal were he not expressing
himself in creative activity. In that case we may regard creation as an
eternal and continuing activity and as one which is meaningful in
God's life and consciousness, including, in particular, that which
involves *our* time.

Probably Augustine suggested the best way of side-tracking what is
at best highly speculative. His dictum was: *"Non in tempore sed cum
tempore, deus fecit mundum."* God did not create the world *in* time but
with time, so that time as we know it belongs to our created order.
Although we can trace back our time scale scientifically to the
initiation of our spatio-temporal order, yet that order did not have a
beginning in time. Even then *our* time must enter into the divine
consciousness.

When we regard absolute creation as *a* divine act, we tend towards deism. This approach so emphasizes the divine transcendence that it regards creation as an initiatory act out of which our universe issued, supplied with the necessary energies, urges and habitual forms of behavior. No further divine interference would have been needed and the thought of divine immanence is to a large extent ignored. Theism, on the other hand, emphasizes both the divine transcendence and the divine immanence. Like panentheism, it regards the whole created order as living, moving and having its being in God, but not as in any sense identified with God since it is created 'out of nothing'. As W. R. Matthews has put it: "The Creator transcends all creatures, not as being one of many or one order among others, but as the active Will in which they take their origin" (*God in Christian Thought and Experience*, London: Nibbet & Co. Ltd., 1935, p. 136).

Creation implies actually both the transcendence and the immanence of God, especially if creation be a continuing and eternal activity of the divine nature. The aspect of transcendence preserves the distinction between God and man. Absolute creation safeguards the discontinuity between God and his creatures. Yet the aspect of immanence is a reminder of the presence of the divine activity within the created order. What God calls into being he also sustains by the energy of his will. It is noteworthy that Augustine could hold that the preservation of the universe could be identified with a continuous creation—since such activity takes place within the order already created and is thus not describable as absolute creation. C. C. J. Webb held that the divine immanence could better be described by the concept of generation (C. C. J. Webb, *God and Personality,* London: George Allen & Universe, 1934, pp. 155ff. I am not in agreement with his reasons but believe that his suggestion is valuable in the use which I am making of it). In this way we can understand the emergence of 'life' and 'mind' in the evolutionary process, and finally the emergence of man. As transcendent intelligent will God calls the whole into being. As personal immanent activity he sustains and directs the process and yet leaves spontaneity to the living organisms and ultimately freedom of decision to the self-conscious spirits as they emerge within the process.

The theistic stance implies that all existent beings have been brought into existence and are being maintained in existence by God's creative will. We cannot describe each moment as a new *creatio ex nihilo*, for there is a continuity, a regularity, a reliability about the behavior of our world. Laws may be regarded as statistical averages, but the mathematical structures which science uses as its models point to a habitual constancy in the world. God gives to nature this stability and reliability. He controls what randomness he permits to it and sets limits to the contingency which it manifests, so that there is in the natural process an overall directiveness. All this means that God's creative activity is immanent in the process, continually communicating being to his creatures. Whatever be the mode of being of his creatures, it is his creative gift to them, whether they be inorganic, organic, low level organisms, mammals possessing consciousness, or human beings with self-consciousness.

Yet this process is still going on. A theistic faith knows the creation was not once for all at the moment of origination of the universe and of our time. It sees a continuing and immanent activity within a process which also has chaotic and contingent elements. The biblical myth begins with a primordial chaos in which God called forth order. Modern cosmogony speaks of an initial explosion of energy as the origination of the universe, and thus tends to introduce a chaotic dimension at the very beginning. To this we must add the view that the orderliness and invariancies which the scientist observes in nature have a statistical basis. Furthermore, at the quantum level of atomic physics, an acausal element is present which the influential Copenhagen school of scientists contends to be ingredient in nature itself and not just bound up with the model and with the limitations inherent in the available experimental apparatus. Thus we face probability and indeterminism within the atomic structure. Finally, the Darwinian and Neo-Darwinian models of evolution have made us very aware of the random aspect in the developmental process of living things. Our Victorian forbears were shocked by the introduction of chance variations. Today we have to live with natural selection and random mutations. Once more we face the presence of contingency. In speaking of God's immanent creative activity within the process, we must take account of this aspect, for often it is the basis for attacks upon the theistic world view.

If God chose to begin with chaos, there must be some purpose behind such a creative act. As science portrays it, the process is one of increasing order and complexity in the evolutionary development towards man. Whatever be the nature of energy, maybe potentially psychical as well as physical, it was so directed by the creative Presence that it produced human freedom. Energy did become knotted into increasingly complex structures within which emerged those higher organizing principles and qualities which we associate with life, mind and spirit. Always the chaotic and contingent elements have been subservient to the forward movement, despite the suffering and evil that has been involved in the warring systems. Such an affirmation says much about the purpose and nature of the Creator. To this we must turn in the next chapters.

Man—
His Nature and Destiny

6 In the last chapter we examined the nature of the creative process and the creative emergence of man. However we may seek to describe scientifically the appearance of man in the long process, it seems clear that here we have what was described in a previous quotation as a 'miracle'. As Teilhard has pointed out, with the coming of man the universe becomes aware of itself. At long last there appears a being who has the capacity of his predecessors to adapt himself to his environment, but also something more. That something more is the ability to understand his environment, to control it and to adapt it to his own ends. Reason and imagination have taken their place upon the world stage. Conscious awareness and an ability to modify instinctive reactions by learning had already betokened the presence of mind. But now self-conscious mind appeared, a capacity to conceptualize and reason, an ability to symbolize and exercise imagination. Above all, we find the presence of will, a capacity to imagine purposes and construct ends and a freedom to pursue them. Undoubtedly such ends were, in the early days, bound up with devising strategies for survival and for dealing with a hostile environment. Yet the evidence for the early presence of religious response to the universe, for rudimentary moral behavior in the formulation of tabus, for primitive beginnings of art in the drawings on the walls of cave-homes—all these remind us of the fact that here was a creature who had concerns for an ideal world as well as the more

realistic ones of dealing with his immediate environment, a being who looked into the future, a creature who was aware of a spiritual order as well as the sensible realm with which he had immediate commerce. As W. H. Thorpe has pointed out, a distinctive feature in the appearance of man upon the earthly scene was a capacity to envisage and pursue absolute values. Truth, beauty, goodness, spiritual concerns now filled the horizon, and higher ends than mere physical and biological survival began to take their place in the behavioral patterns of life on the planet earth.

When Aristotle described man as a rational animal he was putting his finger on one significant aspect of man which made his coming a 'miracle'. To such a description the Hebrew root of our Western culture added the emphasis on will and decision. So together we have a picture of man as a conscious rational being with the freedom to will, able to direct his life and to choose his ends. The pursuits of truth and goodness, conjoined to concern for the beautiful and the holy, lift man above the level of the animal. They present him as a being capable of fellowship with, indeed a mirror image of, the God in whom theistic thought is centered.

Such a view of man is, however, beset by difficulties. Such difficulties are not merely problems but mysteries, using the distinction of Gabriel Marcel. Problems, such as the issues with which science deals, are solvable. Mysteries always remain mysteries, however far we may penetrate into them. Problems belong to the observable, external world of sense experience. Mysteries belong to the inner realm of spiritual experience, the inward dimension of human personality and the invisible spiritual dimension of this vast universe. We may explore such inward depths and so find some light of understanding, but always there are depths beyond that elude our present grasp. And because such depths are beyond the reach of sense observation and experience, they will always be open to skepticism, to mistaken impressions that they are illusory, to rational attempts to explain them away or to reduce them to the level of natural explanation. Such mysteries at the level of human personhood are bound up with the psychosomatic nature of man, the reality of the human spirit or ego, the possibility and nature of freedom, the issue of human survival beyond death. Because man has emerged with the upward movement of the natural process, the human spirit is housed in a mammalian body and rooted in the physical and psychic energies of the lower creatures. Hence when confronted with the mystery of how the self-conscious human spirit is related to the human body and brain, philosophers have always been vexed. It is easy to follow a reductionist method and explain all things in terms of natural forces and urges. The same is true of the closely related issue of the nature and reality of human freedom. It is strangely contradictory and finally irrational to find thinkers employing reason to demonstrate the irrational nature of man and to deny the freedom without which their own reasoning powers could not operate. If reason is unreal, why use reason to demonstrate such a belief!

The Body-Mind Problem and Human Self-Transcendence

Modern science, especially in its medical and psychological branches, is making us very aware of the psychosomatic nature of man. What we call human personality is compounded of the interaction of the inward and the outward in man, the psychical and the physical, the mental and the cerebral, the spiritual and the bodily. We know that physical deficiency or illness has psychical repercussions. If the brain is impaired or the gland secretions are out of balance there may be serious mental accompaniments. Equally, mental disturbances are often associated with physical ills. Thus fear has physical manifestations and so also have other emotional reactions like joy, anger, and grief. Medical investigation has shown long since the effect of mental stress upon blood pressure and the way in which drugs for physical maladies can have mental accompaniments. Furthermore, increasing knowledge has shown the association of various types of mental experience with definite parts of the brain. Often such experiences are impaired when that part of the brain is injured although there is also much evidence that other parts of the brain can sometimes take over the functions of the injured parts.

To this must be added the facts associated with the evolutionary process. The roots of human personality and of its mental life are deep in the long developmental movement out of which man finally emerged. His genetic materials, although distinctive, are yet of the same pattern as those associated with the beginnings of life. The instinctual behavior and sensitivity manifested in early living beings are still present in man. Mental characteristics like the capacity to learn in many higher mammals come to full flower and development in man. Consciousness comes to self-consciousness in human personhood, but awareness is present early in the process of life. Chimpanzees can show some measure of altruism, as if already the roots of human moral consciousness were being implanted in the process. Thus, from the evolutionary point of view, man's self-consciousness and spiritual dimension are grounded in the natural process. His psychosomatic state of being weds him to nature and points to the physical rootage of what theists claim to be his essential nature as self-conscious spirit. It is very evident that for man every mental state tends to run over into a physical and vice versa.

This indicates that there is an affinity between the physical and the psychical such that they are capable of interaction. Ever since Descartes, this idea of interaction has tended to be associated with a radical dualism between mind and matter. Descartes himself gave this dualism a crude form by accepting mind as a substance and giving it a specific location in the pineal gland of the brain, at which point he supposed it to exert an influence upon the body, and, in turn, to be affected by bodily processes. This substantialist kind of thinking has fortunately been left behind and with it the kind of problems which such a radical dualism raises. Today we think in much more dynamic terms. Energy has replaced matter, and psychosomatic wholeness has come to occupy the center of the stage. Whitehead can describe the dualism of mind and matter as an example of the fallacy of misplaced concreteness and can regard the isolation of the physical from the mental as an example of the abstraction associated with analytical reasoning. This can be pressed too far, but whatever matter or physical energy may be (and its nature remains an enigma!), it has the potentiality for bearing mind. The fact already noted that the coming of full self-conscious mind was prepared far down the evolutionary process is an indication that there is an intimate relationship between the mind and the physico-physiological machinery.

We know much more about the brain than Descartes would ever have envisaged. It is accepted that man's conscious mind and mental processes are restricted to that part of the brain known as the cerebral cortex, a thin layer of gray matter sometimes described as the roof brain. Thorpe and others have pointed out that, in contrast to lower organisms, there is, in the case of man, a unitary consciousness. Man's mind functions as a unity, and there is a coordination between the various parts of the brain. Thus specific parts are associated with each sense organ, but the various sensations are received in a way that coordinates their various messages, even though such messages are received in various parts of the cerebral cortex.

The latter is a complicated pattern of intertwining nerve fibers which connect about ten billion nerve cells or neurons. These cells send out impulses or electric discharges. The continuous presence of such exchanges between the nerve cells sets up rapid changes of electric potential which result in characteristic rhythms in the cerebrum. In a relaxed state, a person manifests a steady rhythm, known as the alpha rhythm. Consciousness seems to be associated with irregularity arising in the activity of the neurons. The arrival of a message from some sense organ or some other part of the brain causes a break in the regularity. Consciousness seems to recede when the regularity is restored. Memory is apparently stored up in what have been called 'permanent reverberating circuits' (W. S. Beck, *Modern Science and the Nature of Life*, Camden City, New York: Doubleday & Co., Anchor Books, 1961, p. 297), a cyclic grouping of neurons in which an electric impulse circulates indefinitely. Russell Brain points out that words are associated with electrical patterns in the brain which, when operative, arouse other associated patterns which carry ideas, feelings and memories that convey the meaning of the word for us. Thus the cerebral cortex may be thought of on the model of a highly complex electronic computer.

This analogy must not be pressed too far, although naturalistic reductionism seizes on it and endeavors to eliminate the actuality of the mind. What the study of the brain has done for us is to bring the psychosomatic nature of human personality to a sharp focus. Personality and consciousness are especially bound up with the brain, but other factors are also operative. Nerve centers outside the brain, gland secretions, the state of the hormone cycle—all these may influence human personality as much as the structure of the brain. Hence the computer analogy is at best an *analogy*, and man is not a glorified computer!

It is here that naturalism lifts its head and, in one form or another, contends that man is a product of the natural process, a pattern of physical energy, and nothing more. We have to meet this challenge at the new understanding of the mechanism of the brain. We can argue that electronic computers are human artifacts and that they serve the functions of their makers. They can do only what they are instructed to do. They have to be programmed, and they cannot program themselves. A human brain is self-organizing. It establishes its own patterns of memory and the feedbacks necessary to retain an equilibrium (*vide* S. Zuckerman, "The Mechanising Thought: The Man and the Calculating Machine" in *The Physical Bases of Mind*, edited by Peter Lasless, Oxford: Basil Blackwell, 1957, p. 36). But then we are able to construct computers which have some capacity for establishing and working their own controls, as Zuckerman points out (*ibid.*). We must not set limits to human ingenuity. We may well be able to construct computers which reproduce human feelings and emotions and which, on outward and observable behavior, appear almost human. Even then, however, naturalism can be countered.

For one thing, what is distinctive in human personality is its inner side—its 'I-ness'. Outwardly I may be described as a 'he', and my conduct may be simulated by a computer. But inwardly I know that I know, I know that I *have* emotions, I am self-aware. When someone is unconscious and does not respond to stimuli, like I do, I know that he is not like 'I' in an important way. The objective language of science does not fully describe or explain the 'I' whom I know from within. As I. T. Ramsey comments: "whether we could say that the machines 'had' emotions as we might say 'I had' the emotions, is the point at issue. Could a machine display genuine, that is self-disclosed, ownership?" (I. T. Ramsey, *Religion and Science: Conflict and Synthesis*, London: S.P.C.K., 1964, p. 59).

A second point also needs to be made. The naturalist presupposes that the only way of knowing is the empirical and objectifying way characteristic of the scientific method. But we have argued that such an analytic approach ignores the primary and intuitive awareness of wholes and its development in the knowledge that comes through love and sympathy. This is the way that we come to know and understand other minds, other 'I's'. Paul Weiss, in a searching analysis, argues that though one might, on the ground of behavior, attribute minds to machines which behave like oneself, yet they are not human. They fail on two counts—they cannot be loved by one who can love and they cannot love what can be loved. He writes: "a machine is an artifact whose parts are united so as to enable them to act together, whereas man is a unity in which the whole governs the behavior of the parts. Only such a unity has a self, with feelings, mind, will, and the rest" (P. Weiss, "Love in a Machine Age," *Dimensions of Mind*, edited by S. Hook, New York: Collier Books, 1961, p. 180). The same resort is made in this argument to the inner and subjective aspect of the 'I', which can be penetrated only by love and by the 'I's' capacity to love in response. Furthermore, there is the differentiation made earlier between an aggregate of parts and a whole. There is something more, some holistic factor, which violates any attempt to turn an analogy into an identity.

One contemporary naturalistic attempt to avoid the kind of duality we are implying is the so-called identity theory of H. Feigl, U.T. Place and J. J. C. Smart. They hold that there is not a separate class of mental events distinct from the physiological events in the brain. There is no internal screen, no phenomenal field, on which images of objects and events are cast. Every mental event is identical with some state of the brain. Feigl contends that we have a body-mind identity, in which the neuro-physiological terms and the corresponding phenomenal terms, though they differ widely in sense or meaning, yet have identical referents. (*vide* H. Feigl, "Mind-Body, Not a Pseudo-Problem" in *Dimensions of Mind, op. cit.*, pp. 33-42). Place likewise dismisses the "assumption that if the meanings of two statements or expressions are quite unconnected, they cannot provide an adequate characterization of the same object or state of affairs" (U. T. Place, "Is Consciousness a Brain Process?" in *The Philosophy of Mind*, edited by V. C. Chappell, Englewood Cliffs, N. J.: Prentice-Hall, 1962, p. 103). In this way such naturalistic thinkers seek to avoid an idea of metaphysical transcendence. Consciousness *is* a process of the brain. Mental statements and physiological descriptions have the same referents, events in the brain.

Such views do, at any rate, avoid the other naturalistic approach— epiphenomenalism. According to this view, the consciousness merely reflects the processes in the brain and does not initiate them. The causative process is one-sided. Only the physiological processes can initiate causal connections, and the mind is reduced to a manifestation of the physical. Like a mirror, consciousness shows what is happening in the somatic and cerebral processes. The mental states are dependent variables, connected with the physiological and observable phenomena but not causing them. The contemporary investigation of parapsychological phenomena does offer at least enough verifiable evidence to indicate that the understanding of the human mind is not dependent wholly on physical and physiological principles. Telepathy points to mind being more than an epiphenomenon. It also calls in question the identity theory just discussed. We can find no evidence of some cerebral receiving and transmitting center through which physical radiation could provide communication with other personal beings. Sir Charles Sherrington aptly expressed his own lifetime experiences as an investigator: "nothing known of mind brings mind within what we conceive as energy. Mind refuses to be energy, just as it has always refused to be matter" (C. Sherrington, *Man on His Nature*, Cambridge: Cambridge University Press, 1946, p. 348).

Gilbert Ryle has taken up the identity theory at the linguistic level and given it a distinctive twist. He holds that the fallacy of Cartesian dualism is one of category. The word 'mind' does not refer to a thing, but it and cognate terms are simply a description of certain types of human behavior. Thus a description in mental terms and a description in physical terms have different meanings, but they both refer to the same physical process. Ryle does not concern himself with the physiological processes of the cerebrum as do the preceding thinkers. He concentrates on the outward, observable somatic behavior. His thesis is, however, very like theirs. There are no mental processes as distinct from physical processes. Any immaterial thinking substance such as mind is a fiction. Even self-awareness has no inner aspect. For Ryle, it arises from listening to our own words and studying our own behavior and is thus not distinguishable from knowledge of other people.

John Wisdom attacks Ryle by pointing out that the peculiarity of the soul is not that it is visible to none but that it is visible only to one. This, Wisdom contends, need not lead to skepticism about knowledge of other minds. This knowledge is a fact and thus telepathy has to be considered.

Ryle points to the "elusiveness of the I" and thus dismisses mind as "the ghost in the machine," however non-objectifiable and not clearly definable the 'I' is. The myth of mind still remains to haunt him. H. D. Lewis cogently remarks that the proneness of Professor Ryle's 'ghost' to make a fresh appearance at the moment it has been thought to be finally laid is not, as some suppose, merely because it has been built into the structure of our language or is unavoidable in descriptions of overt behavior, but because we are directly aware of ourselves as non-material beings, and there is also involved in this a quite irreducible difficulty of knowing what it is like or means to be another mind. (H. D. Lewis, "God and Mystery" in *Prospect for Metaphysics*, edited by Ian Ramsey, London: George Allen & Unwin, 1961, pp. 208ff.).

All these theories, however refined, offer brands of reductionist naturalism. Ryle concentrates on the overt physical behavior whereas the identity thinkers are concerned with the physiological processes of the brain, but each in his own way would deny any distinct substantial status to mind. Man still remains a mystery, however, and the reality of his spiritual/mental aspect refuses to be swept away. There is an aspect of transcendence in man which defies reduction to the physical and physiological.

So we return to the issue of man's psychosomatic wholeness and its duality of the mental and the physical. We do not have to accept the Cartesian dualism of incompatibles, for, as we have already indicated, the mind has emerged within and been closely associated with the increasingly complex patterns of physical energy. Mind and brain have grown up together. Mind has its roots deep down in the physical and physiological aspects of man's bodily structure. Furthermore the coming of mind was anticipated in the increasing complexity of the patterns into which the physical energy became knotted in the evolutionary process. Indeed, as we have already seen, it would seem as if the coming of life was the shaping of rudimentary mind. It would appear that mind was a potential dimension of energy from the very beginning, so that energy was never purely physical but carried, in nascent form, another and mental aspect.

The fact that mind has emerged within the physical patterning of the process by no means supports the idea that mind is a refined manifestation of the physical order. To say this is to fall into the fallacy attacked centuries ago by Aristotle—that of identifying an entity with its origins rather than its ends. That mind emerges from matter and discloses by its thought a rational order in the physical realm might conversely suggest the hidden but organizing presence of mind from the beginning. We have just as much justification for adopting this teleological approach as the naturalistic reductionist position.

Indeed, when the naturalist seizes upon the feedback mechanical brain to support his contention, he is forgetting that such a mechanism is the creation of thinking men and that its direction is dictated by the purpose for which it is made. Even at the level of the artifact, mind in its creative and directing capacity is a necessity. We find the same state of affairs in a living organism, for such an organism is a temporal process in which the "befores" are drawn up into and included within the "afters," rather than being mere causative antecedents. A. A. Bowman suggests that "the movement of life is not like the movement of a projectile in space, but like that of a snowball gathering substance as it goes" (*The Sacramental Universe*, Princeton: Princeton University Press, 1939, p. 363). What in an earlier chapter we have called, using Polanyi's terminology, the organizing principle of life has taken charge. Energy is being organized in a way that prepares it to serve the capacities of mind and spirit. The time form of an organism is directed forward and is capable, therefore, of bearing meaning. Life provides the spatiotemporal patterned structure of physical energy within which mind and ultimately human personality may flower. When mind does make its presence evident, already physical energy has been adapted to enter into functional relationship with it. Bowman suggests that life transforms the time of physics into the time of life, characterized by the distinction of past, present and future. Thereby a living body is being fitted to enter into "a single ontological (even though heterogeneous) system with the spiritual mode of being, and to be the vehicle for the moral purposes of mankind" (*ibid*, p. 363).

Man is a whole, a single system, howbeit imperfect. The two components of the physical and the mental are always within that whole. We have a duality but not a dualism, cooperative and not incompatible. We use the word 'person' to describe man in his wholeness. He *has* a mind and a physical body. He *is* a person. In that personhood or selfhood the duality of the physical and the mental is integrated at the level of self-conscious mind or spirit. He is an 'I', an ego, a subject. He is spirit. Harold K. Schelling reminds us of the way in which we describe persons as 'dispirited'. He notes that 'spirit' cannot be clearly and objectively defined. But that is to be expected, for spirit is never an object. It is always subject; it is equivalent to 'I'-ness. As Schelling suggests: "in the case of spirit ... we feel ourselves to be in strange territory" (H. K. Schelling, *The New Consciousness in Science and Religion*, Philadelphia: United Church Press, 1973, p. 152). 'Spirit' is man's unique quality. It is more even than mind. He *has* a mind, but he *is* spirit. Spirit describes the unique wholeness or 'I'-ness of man, his self-awareness, his subjectivity.

Buber defines spirit as "man's totality that has become consciousness, the totality which comprises and integrates all his capacities, powers, qualities and urges" (M. Buber, *Israel and the World*, New York: Schocken Books, 1948, p. 175). In other words, all the physical, biological, and mental factors are brought to a focus in self-awareness. Man is not just a higher mammal. He is a subject, with all that the word implies. He is in the objective order, and he may be described at that level, for he is somatic. But he transcends that order, for he is the one who knows, controls and orders it. Of man, more than all creatures, it may be said that there is a within and a without, and that the within, the subjective, is the focal, dominant and integrating aspect of his being.

Only of man can we use two language categories. We can describe him objectively in terms of his bodily behavior—"He is doing something." Or we can describe him in terms of his mental and inner life—"He is thinking." In the first case, what is said comes from direct observation and is public. In the second case, what is said is the result of either inference or of direct communication from the person concerned. It is private and remains only to the person whose inner life it is. One is the language of observation and the other is the language of experience.

These two languages are bound together by the personal pronoun "I"—"I am doing something" and "I am thinking" describe respectively the outer or somatic and the inner or mental aspect of personal being. The subjective "I" binds them together. If the "I" is replaced by "he," the inner world is no longer open to the speaker. The inner world of motivation, emotion, reasons, free choice is closed to all observers. 'I' can experience but others can only observe. I. T. Ramsey points out that "a first person singular activity word tells of more than 'objects'" for "my 'free' activity is more than the public behavior which expresses it" (I. T. Ramsey, *Freedom and Immortality*, London: S. C. M. Press, 1960, p. 87). The word "I" describes that personal whole where brain/body and mind meet.

"I" is elusive and hence Ryle could dismiss it as the ghost in the machine. 'I' cannot be expressed in objective categories, for 'he' is always less than 'I'. 'I' indeed makes objective sentences logically odd. "I am asleep" and "I am dead" are logically hybrid for 'asleep' and 'dead' are objective categories, their meaning is bound up with objects such as 'he'. The peculiarity of 'I' in the epistemological process is that it is always the knowing subject, even in introspection. As a consequence it is never able to turn self into an object. What knows is always marked off from what is known by an uncrossable barrier. I always put myself over against that which I seek to know and to express objectively.

There can be no object without a subject, a personal observer, and that subject can never be included in the object. Even when I turn my body into an object, the body becomes an abstraction from what, following van Peursen, we might call our bodiliness. The 'I' still remains as subject, and its state in the world is its bodiliness. My bodiliness makes objectivity possible, even when I abstract 'body' from its wholeness and make it an object. Always my subjectivity transcends my world of objective fact. As van Peursen has written:

> the body must never be construed as a given object because there is more in it than that: it is 'lived', experienced body, structured from a source, that is, from the standpoint of the subject. The *body* considered as an object is derivative, is inferred from body as inalienable center; and it is the latter to which we refer in speaking of the body as 'bodiliness' (C. A. van Peursen, *Body, Soul, and Spirit: A Survey of the Body-Mind Problem*. London: Oxford University Press, 1966, p. 172).

When I refer to my subjective 'I'-ness, spirit, I am speaking of my personal wholeness with its bodiliness.

The subjective/objective dichotomy also applies to self-knowledge. It holds for my empirical ego, my own 'he'-ness. I think about myself thinking, and going deeper, I think about myself thinking about myself thinking, and so on. 'I' always eludes me in this dimension of knowing. I know myself *as knowing*. I know my inner activity but I do not know 'I'. The self that I know is never identical with 'I', for I am also the one who knows. I am both knower and known, and thus there is in every 'I' the quality of self-transcendence. 'I' am always more than I comprehend, and 'he' is always less than 'I'.

In the dimension of self-awareness, although aware of myself intuitively or tacitly, I cannot define exactly what consciousness is. There is a *sui generis* quality which makes it irreducible to or not expressible in subjective or physical categories. 'I' includes my body and its physiological machinery and my mental states, but 'I' also transcends them. My apprehension of my self is an apprehension that cannot be fully expressed.

Recalling our earlier differentiation between problem and mystery, we are here dealing with mystery. In much of our experience at the personal and suprapersonal levels we are concerned with mysteries which can only be penetrated by disclosure and sympathetic imagination and even then mystery remains. We can no more grasp the 'I' of the other person than we can grasp our own. We may label him as an object and adopt the impersonal objectifying approach to him. Then we concern ourselves only with what is observable and dismiss his inner personal being. Or we may involve ourselves with him and seek, to use Marcel's phrase, to participate in the mystery of his being. (G. Marcel, *The Mystery of Being, I. Reflection and Mystery*, London: The Harvil Press, Ltd., 1950, especially pp. 197ff.) For mystery he is, and mystery he remains, even when, from his own personal disclosure and by our own sympathetic imagination, we have sought to understand him. We can give no clear and distinct statement about his consciousness any more than we can give one of our own.

Buber points out that directly we turn the other into an object the reality of the 'thou' evades us as it does with ourselves, for we set the other at a distance from us (cf. M. Friedmann, *Martin Buber: The Life of Dialogue*, Chicago: University of Chicago Press, 1955, pp. 80ff). He holds that such a distance is necessary if relation is to be possible. It differentiates us from the other and so opens the way to relationship. Personal involvement at the level of disclosure needs to alternate with the objective way of knowing. It is inevitable that we should withdraw from the personal involvement of the 'I-Thou' relation to the objective contemplation of the 'I-It' relation. Yet we can never understand the Thou if we remain in the latter. We depersonalize the Thou and thereby depersonalize ourselves. Erich Frank suggests that "as long as man interprets himself merely in terms of objective nature and shapes his life and his world according to this concept, he estranges himself from his real self, and his soul becomes empty" (Erich Frank, *Philosophical Understanding and Religious Truth*, New York: Oxford University Press, 1945, p. 15).

This statement reminds us that our own self-awareness is only fully realized as we are actually involved with the other in personal relationship. It would appear that self-consciousness comes to birth in us along with the consciousness of others. Buber reminds us that "individuality makes its appearance by being differentiated from other individualities. A person makes his appearance by entering into relation with other persons" (M. Buber, *I and Thou*, translated by R. Gregor Smith, Edinburgh: T. & T. Clarke, 1937, p. 62). The antenatal life of the child rests in the womb of the mother. As the child develops, so this relationship, at the level of spirit, differentiates into self-consciousness and consciousness of the 'Thou'. Buber can say: "I become through my relation to the *Thou*; as I become I, I say *Thou*" (*ibid*, p. 11).

The key to the mystery of the other is love. It is by love that we become truly involved with other persons and spirit may meet spirit. The other comes to us always in a personal disclosure in which claim and sympathy are commingled. He or she challenges us to involvement. The 'Thou' calls on us to forsake the enthronement of our own personhood in an objectified world which we seek to order and control. We are bidden to be open to the other. Love, commitment and responsible decision are evoked.

It is here that the theistic understanding of man reaches its full expression and that man can achieve his full destiny. For if free personhood is attained through relation to other persons, it must reach its full expression in relation to a personal God. Man experiences the presence and claims of God through the relationships to other persons and to his world. Our very environment, natural and social/personal, calls us into encounter with the encompassing reality, God. And once more we face mystery. For if our personal self-transcendence leaves personhood veiled in mystery, how much more the nature of a personal God. If we cannot clearly express human personhood how much less clearly can we express God's nature, the infinite Spirit who hides himself in his transcendence and yet touches our lives in his immanence. Indeed, our own personal self-transcendence can help us to understand both the openness and hiddenness of God.

It is at this level of disclosure that man exercises both the rational and moral dimensions of his consciousness. Disclosure involves communication, and the signal mode of communication is words or language. Even some higher mammals communicate to some degree by signs, and here we may see the evolutionary preparation for the emergence of self-conscious, self-transcendent spirit. Man is a rational being, and closely bound up with this is his symbolizing ability. Somewhere and mysteriously, where self-conscious mind and cerebral cortex express their unity, a symbolizing process goes on. Sensations become apprehensions, apprehensions are conceptualized, and man's symbolizing ability takes over. He is not only conscious of messages from his world, but he is also able to put them at a distance, to order and compare them, to formulate concepts which have been freed from any particular perceptual situation, and to organize his bodily signs, including sounds in speech, so that these may become communicative symbols to his fellows. His rationality goes step in step with his symbolizing capacity. He is a maker of language, and so he gives his reason full scope. By his words he organizes and symbolizes his experiences and communicates them to other minds. He transcends his signs so that he is able to develop them grammatically and order their usage. Man's capacity for free ideas, his gift for rational ordering and critical judgment, his ability to symbolize and communicate by language are all facets of one aspect of his self-transcendence—his ability to find meaning in his world.

Man as a Moral Being—Freedom and Determinism

When W. H. Thorpe defined man as a being who can appraise absolute values, he was placing his finger upon one essential distinctive. Man is a being who finds a meaning for his existence which transcends the natural. He is able to rise above the issues of physical survival and choose a deeper meaning for existence. He is aware of depths in his environment which mere natural forces cannot account for. He is a religious being, aware of an infinite Presence, and he is a moral being, responsive to ethical claim and bearing responsibility for his behavior. Now all this implies decision, choice, basic freedom. Man is a free and responsible being.

It is here that naturalism again lifts its head. 'Scientism' or naturalistic psychology seeks to explain away man's feeling for absolute values and to undermine his freedom. As we have seen, it takes the scientific evidence and makes man into a causative structure. Mind is either another way of talking about the causative process of the cerebrum or it is an epiphenomenon cast around the cortex, reflecting and not influencing the processes. Freedom is thus denied, and man's vision of the good is reduced to purely material origins.

In science we are dealing with means and not ends, with the instrument and not with the purposes that may activate it, with efficient causation and not with teleogical. The instrument—physical, physiological and even psychological—can have no purpose of its own. The purpose belongs to the directing agent. We should expect the instrument to possess its own determinate character, if it is to be effective in the service of the 'I'. If we abstract bodily and psychological processes out of our "bodiliness" and objectify them, we should expect such a determinate character to be manifest, for freedom remains ever in the depths of subjectivity, of 'I'. Furthermore, what we so objectify has already happened and what cannot be objectified is our own inner agency, its subjective dimension. Like a cinematograph film, we see it crystallized, objectified, set in pattern, after the event. It comes to us objectified with an emphasis on its befores, whereas we directly experience it in terms of its aims. The objective picture presents efficient causation, whereas subjectively there is a teleological aspect. Science may analyze the psychological forces at work in moral decision and reduce our free and responsible act to the level of determinism, but thereby it ignores our own immediate experience, with its vision of the good, with its awareness of moral ends, with its basic feeling of freedom and responsibility, with its sense of personal backing.

This picture holds of personal introspection, but it also holds of other persons whom we may study objectively. Insofar as they voluntarily become the instruments of our intentions, we may expect to find a determinate character in their behavior. This is the basis of all propaganda, suggestion techniques, and brain washing tactics—to impose ideas upon the other which will determine his intentions; even more dangerously, to loosen in some way the contact between inner freedom and the objectifiable instrument so that the other becomes a means to our ends.

At the psychological level, we have considerable preoccupation with the denial of freedom and the enthronement of determinism. The disciples of Freud admit the presence of mind as a product of natural forces but place all their emphasis upon the nature of the unconscious. They turn consciousness into something that is entirely determined by hidden forces in the jungle of the unconscious, especially sex and aggressiveness. They present a picture of man as a creature who, at every level of his being, is determined by the natural forces that are involved in his personal structure. Freedom is an illusion. The conscience, which Kant had made the keystone of such freedom, is at best but a superego thrown up by unresolved conflicts which have been repressed into the unconscious. Man's behavior is thus a reflection of natural impulses determined by unconscious forces. Even his reasoning is simply rationalization, an attempt to find reasons for behavior which is totally determined by the unconscious.

The early behaviorism and its concern with conditioned reflexes have been modified considerably by naturalistic thinkers. We have already looked at the identity thinkers and also at Gilbert Ryle, but a much more direct attack upon the reality of human freedom is found in contemporary work of B. F. Skinner. The assumption is made that scientific methodology offers the sole way to knowledge, and hence that such aspects of personal experience as freedom, moral obligation and religious vision can be regarded as reactions due to appropriate conditioning. We find here a new psychological form of scientism.

B. F. Skinner, a professor at Harvard, has experimented with animals and made the, for him, easy transition from the behavior of animals to that of man. His fundamental premise is the naturalistic one that men are animals and are to be understood on a machine-like model. His emphasis is on the relation of an animal to its environment. A certain kind of behavior, such as a rat pressing on the bars of its cage, is conditioned when this activity is met by a morsel of food. Because such 'operant' behavior produces such consequences, the animal is stimulated to repeat it. Thus Skinner's experiments are concerned with the effect on behavior of environmental rewards and punishments. Although authoritative, these investigations are so limited in scope that there is little justification for their universal application to the human species. Yet Skinner does just this. He states dogmatically, with little or no argumentative support, that since the causative method applies on the physical and animal level, it must apply with equal certainty to man himself. What must be done in order "to save man" is to manipulate the human environment so that satisfactory behavior is evoked.

Skinner asserts that "the man that man has devised is the product of the culture that man has devised" (B. F. Skinner, *Beyond Freedom and Dignity*, New York: Bantam/Vintage Books, 1972, p. 198). He thus rejects the traditional view and boldly declares that man, as a member of a species, has been shaped by evolutionary contingencies and manifested behavioral tendencies which have brought him under the control of both his natural and social/cultural environment. For Skinner, the scientific view is that "man does not act on the world, the world acts on him" (*ibid*, p. 202). His scheme calls for a wholesale 'scientific' renovation of man's cultural milieu. He arrogantly believes that his analysis of human behavior and his technique of cultural conditioning are universal, applicable to all men everywhere. Thus he believes that all men can be conditioned to produce behavior appropriate to the well-being of themselves and their fellows.

Such inner feelings as freedom and dignity, a sense of responsibility and self-respect, faith and a sense of purpose must be dismissed. Mind, will, character traits have no place in Skinner's thought. His ground for dismissing them would appear to be that "there is nothing like it in modern physics or most of biology." Once more this naturalistic presupposition creeps through. There is nothing unique about man. What applies to the animal applies to him, and the idea of a distinctive 'human nature' must be eliminated. The responsibility must be shifted from the 'inner man' to the environment.

One might well ask why, if all behavior, including presumably thought and writing, is conditioned by the cultural environment, Skinner is convinced that his approach is the correct one. This question becomes more cogent when we note that he rejects our contemporary culture and its views as traditional. Then presumably his own writing has not been conditioned by his culture, and his book is a denial of his fundamental position! One has the feeling that we have here a faked-up case which is one gigantic deception based on false assumptions, though plausibly written.

Again, Skinner writes as if all the behavioristic technique is planned and available for introducing his new culture, although he admits that traditional views in society would make its institution difficult. But it is by no means clear that the analysis of human behavior at this cultural level has passed much beyond a very rudimentary stage with Skinner and his cohorts!

Furthermore Skinner, like all behaviorists, dismisses the inner side of man. As we have already noted, the scientist qua scientist cannot take account of what is not theoretically observable. This, however, does not rule out areas of experience, including our own subjectivity, which are not subject to scientific methodology. After all, even science itself is the product of that human mind which apparently Skinner, himself a competent scientist, would deny.

Finally, who is to be the happy innovator of the new cultural situation and on what evaluational basis is he to act? To speak of a benevolent dictator may be well, but what is the 'good' at which he aims? Here we fall back on the well-worn chestnut of Waddington and others that what is good is what makes for the survival of the race. What in the evolutionary development of the race have come to be regarded as 'goods' should be used as rewards to induce people to behave for the 'good of others' (*ibid.*, p. 120). When we ask what is the 'good of others', the answer appears to be ultimately survival. "Survival is the only value according to which a culture is eventually to be judged, and any practice that furthers survival has survival value by definition" (*ibid.*, p. 130).

But surely personal fulfillment is more important than personal or racial survival. Even our mass media are in continual search for personal meaning. Questions, variously phrased, raise the questions 'Who am I?', 'What am I here for?', and one popular song used to declare: "I want to be me." The whole postulate of survival reflects the naturalism which is basic to Skinner's thought.

Once we have banished the kind of determinism which is a very present challenge to the validity of our experience of freedom, we must still seek to examine and justify what freedom is. Teilhard argued that the understanding of the whole process of evolution was incomplete unless it included man with all his rich variety of responses and most of all his capacity to love. Hence he called for a metascience which included not just what the natural sciences could grasp by their scientific method, but also that inner side of the whole process which comes to full flower in human self-awareness. He wanted to use the word 'physics' in the special sense of "a systematic comprehension of all nature." For him those qualities which we label 'spiritual' also belong to any general construction of the world, and certainly to the understanding of man. C. F. Mooney cites a statement of Teilhard that we have "still no science of the universe including man as such. Present day physics ... as yet makes no place for thought; which means it is still constructed wholly apart from the most remarkable of all phenomena provided by nature for our observation" (C. F. Mooney, *Teilhard de Chardin and the Mystery of Christ*, New York: Harper & Row, Publishers, 1966, p. 27). We would add that human freedom finds no place either in science and that science ignores any suggestion of a meta-science especially because of positivistic influences.

Empirically, of course, we observe only behavior. Psychological scientism, in staying there, is strictly scientific, but that is no justification for avoiding the further investigation which the inner side of the process requires. Freedom belongs to the inner side of personality. It is private, not publicly observable. If we start, like the scientist, from the empirical standpoint we have to ask what constitutes a situation in which freedom and responsibility are experienced by the subject. We can be grateful for the careful analysis undertaken by I. T. Ramsey (*Freedom and Immortality*, London: S. C. M. Press, 1960, especially the first two chapters). At the moment of free decision, there is present something more than the mere objective behavior pattern—the transcendent aspect of personal being associated with 'I', spirit. 'I' know that I am not limited to an objective behavior which is evident to a scientific observer. The chemical, reflexive, instinctive, inhibitive, and unconscious movements and urges which he analyzes are all transcended. In my free decision I realize myself as something more than the causal sequences which scientific language describes. As Ramsey puts it: "My behavior, to me, when deliberate or decisive, is 'objects' *and more*" (*ibid.*, p. 28). Thus events might outwardly fit completely into a causative framework, so that my activity may appear to be the result of causes beyond myself. Yet, even in such events, I can declare that they have "my backing" and that they express my decisive activity.

There is a difference between what we may call social behavior and what may be described as moral behavior, between mores and ethics. Skinner has not faced the fact that a complex situation may evoke different responses in people. It is just here that Ramsey's analysis is enlightening. Some may respond by mere conformance to the social pattern, but others may respond in a more responsible way and exercise their freedom in so doing. Often the latter conduct may also manifest the accepted pattern; sometimes it will not. Yet whatever be the pattern of conduct, it will have my personal "backing." It will be mine, an expression of my subjectivity and realization of my 'I'-ness. No scientific conditioning can include this aspect of subjective "backing" in its understanding, and Skinner has of course omitted it completely—it is not scientifically observable. Social performance only becomes moral behavior when such personal backing is involved. The conduct is really *mine*.

From the moral and religious point of view, including the theistic, no description purely in terms of causal events will ever be adequate. Such a standpoint claims that the sense of responsibility implies freedom to choose. If I have an obligation, then I also have the capacity to evade it. We are not creatures under compulsion from efficient causation, but we have the gift of *responsible* decision.

Ramsey sees a dual aspect in the transcendent dimension of such a moral situation. One aspect is outward and the other is inward. The outward aspect is the awareness of a transcendent claim which rises beyond the customary behavior or usual responses and makes us aware of a challenging Presence. Thus the good Samaritan might have ignored the injured Jew, conforming to the behavioral pattern expected by his group. The situation would have been impersonal. It became moral and personal when he became aware of his responsibility to another human being, not just a Jew. Transcendent claim was laid upon him, and the situation became personal and moral.

The second aspect is the subjective one—a responsible free decision which transcends the normally expected public behavior. It is conduct which rises above any "specific determination." A "natural" or "impersonal" act will be causally connected with and determined by the objective situation alone. But in free decision there is no restraint expressible in causal language. Thus a man may decide to get married because of circumstances. He may want a wife to "see him through college," or he may decide to marry money and relieve himself of pecuniary embarrassment. There is here an external causative structure—college education or lack of funds. On the other hand, he may marry because he sees something worthy of his total commitment and love in the woman. In such a decision he freely decides to marry and to accept the obligation which such commitment brings with it and which is expressed in the marriage vows. Outwardly the behavior will appear the same, but an impersonal, causative act will give place to a personal and responsible decision.

The crux of truly personal moral behavior thus turns upon man's freedom. It lies in the reality of his 'I', of human spirit, of personal subjectivity. The 'I' has a sense of obligation as it discerns a certain moral claim in the objective situation and makes a free and responsible decision in the light of the claim. As Ramsey remarks, "the determination of my decision when there is free will, is no causal determination. It is a peculiar kind of response to a peculiar kind of challenge" (*ibid.*, p. 38).

The emphasis on freedom has characterized the existentialist school of thinkers. Rebelling against determinism of any form, Hegelian idealistic, Marxist materialistic or naturalistic, they have directed philosophic thought to a serious consideration of the nature of man and the issue of philosophical anthropology. Their emphasis has been so strongly anthropological that often they have not presented any ontological development and, at least in the case of Kierkegaard, have even shunned it. However, thinkers like Tillich, Marcel, Jaspers and Heidegger have sought to develop an ontological understanding which includes their existentialist emphasis.

The existentialist turns to the inner bastions of personal being and declares man's essential freedom. For him, the distinctive mark of man is his freedom and responsibility. He is realistic in his analysis of man's somatic state and of his natural and social environment. He recognizes man's historicity, his position in space and time. He offers no retreat to any idealistic ivory tower. Man is characterized by his 'thrownness'. He is here and not there. He is now and not then. His life is marked by birth, by death, by temporal transience. He is limited by his somatic condition, by his social pressures, by his historical placing. He is not unconditioned. Yet within this area he is free to determine his existence.

As here used, 'existence' has a peculiarly distinctive meaning. It expresses man's free decision about the nature of his personal being. Christian existentialists, such as Kiekegaard, Marcel and Tillich, argue that man's essential being is ontologically prior to any decision on his part. This is the general theistic position, for man is related to God, and his choice may lead to the actualization of his true nature or it may lead to an existence which is estranged from his true nature. Atheistic existentialists like Sartre and Camus would hold that each person determines his own being in his existential choice, taking cognizance of his situation.

All emphasize the centrality of freedom, decision and responsibility. The categories which they employ are inevitably associated with the inner aspect of personal being. They speak of responsibility and guilt, of fear and finitude. They bid man look downwards into his innermost being and consider the decision that he must make in the deeps of his spirit. The pressure of conscience, the anguish and sense of guilt which beset man, his conditioned nature, his finitude and historicity call for decision. In the light of his 'thrownness' in space and time and under the claim of the Unconditioned, the Transcendent Encompassing, the divine Presence, he must decide what kind of man he is going to be. Transcendent claim without and the inner capacity to rise above causative factors in free and responsible decision—these elements are present.

For theistic thinkers the transcendent claim is paramount. Once such an existential choice has been made and a person has decided his or her destiny, the commitment is reflected in every subsequent choice. A person may decide what kind of person to be, for or against the divinely given destiny, and that choice will set the direction of inner personhood. This means that our inner decisions are not indeterminate. The freedom of which we are speaking is not indetermination. A man discerns a certain pattern in the objective order and apprehends a personal presence which lays claim upon him and which challenges him to responsive love. As he commits himself in free decision at this point, he finds his true freedom in doing God's will. Such commitment determines his character, the central direction of 'I'. Around it are increasingly integrated all his psychosomatic urges, and the forces of his life tend to flow along channels which become more and more habitual. His specific acts of choice may vary, but their general kind will be in line with that continuity of personal being, character, which the primal existential choice has directed. His personal being becomes increasingly integrated and reflects his inner commitment. Within that initial commitment he remains free and responsible, but this freedom is not mere indetermination. It bears a strong element of self-determination. It reflects his inner being, and the less integrated he is, the less dependable will his decisions be. Ramsey's analysis has been followed in the discussion in this paragraph, and he leaves it open at just this point. William Temple reminds us that "freedom is not absence of determination; it is spiritual determination, as distinct from mechanical or even organic determination. It is determination by what seems good as contrasted with determination by irresistible compulsion" (W. Temple, *Nature, Man and God*, New York: The Macmillan Co., 1956, p. 229).

Such a decision is not a universal one. Man may refuse to be a singular one, a true person—to use Kierkegaard's phrase. Man's historical state is not one of conscious and acknowledged relation to God. As Kierkegaard saw it, he may live at the level of desire, in which case he chooses a naturalistic mode of existence, and such a choice will mean the enslavement of his freedom. His 'will' will be subject to lower desires, and the challenge of the higher in *most* situations will be rejected. He may, at a higher level, center his life in himself or determine his existence by commitment to certain moral principles. Yet the mystery is always that his existence remains ego-centered. He is placing himself or his natural urges and desires in the place of God. He either regards himself as self-sufficient or he merges himself in his natural environment. In so doing he becomes alienated from his true destiny as a moral and spiritual being existing in relation to God. He turns his world into an instrument to serve his own purposes. He regards his fellows as means to his ends, not as ends in themselves. So we come to moral evil and the mystery of man's mishandled freedom. To this issue we must turn in the next chapter.

The Issue of Human Survival Beyond Death— Immortality or Resurrection?

We turn now to the issue of man's ultimate destiny. The theist, believing in a personal God and in the supreme value of human personality, is concerned with survival beyond death. Holding to the personal as the highest created value and regarding it as supremely expressed in God himself, he regards immortality as an essential characteristic of man. The divine purpose for man is not completed at death but is directed towards final fulfillment in some dimension other than our creaturely space and time. The human reason seeks to reinforce such an affirmation of religious faith by constructing some rational substructure which might point to its reasonableness.

We must at once note that although the idea of personal survival beyond death is widespread and persistent in the religious consciousness, it is by no means universal. Furthermore, the naturalistic challenge lifts its head again, chiefly at the level of the body/mind relationship. We must look at this first since it is very contemporary.

It is argued that the failure of memory under certain psychological conditions, or when the brain is injured, or when old age degenerates the tissues around the cerebral cortex, is positive evidence that the memory depends upon cerebral processes. Hence death must result in the utter disappearance of thought and therefore in the end of human existence. On this view, consciousness is a function of the brain, an emergent due to a certain pattern of organic cells, and without a brain to function there can be no consciousness.

C. D. Broad took the view that mentality is an emergent characteristic and not a differentiating attribute, holding that consciousness is only able to function when associated with a brain. He did not, however, adopt the naturalistic path. His realism allowed him to accept the reality of mind. Hence his interest in psychical investigations even led him towards some idea of survival. He argued that there is, in human personality, a psychical factor which constitutes the 'emergent characteristic' and which only functions as 'mind' in relation to a brain. After death this psychical factor persists for some time apart from the brain. This is capable of associating itself with the brains of mediums and thus gives rise to mind. Broad noted that psychical messages are usually asssociated with those whose death is recent, and hence he holds that the existence of this psychic factor is only temporary. He did at least suggest that, in some way, the psychic factor carries memory since, when associated with a strange brain, it can stimulate this brain to report memories of the original personality. This view is also a reminder that persistence after death does not necessarily imply immortality. This theory is not strongly based, but it shows that realism does not inevitably mean naturalism.

The naturalistic challenge does, however, require us to look at Broad's differentiation between mentality as an emergent characteristic and mentality as a differentiating attribute. We have contended that mentality has been potentially present in the process from the beginning and that physical energy has been sufficiently akin to life and mind to carry this higher dimension of being until the right conditions were obtained for the full emergence of man as spirit. By taking this position and connecting it with a holistic understanding of man as personal spirit, we have argued that the emergence of man is a 'miracle', the coming of a new level of reality utterly distinct from, yet having its roots in, the lower levels. Human spirit or personality is a differentiating attribute, which transcends the physical, vital, and mental levels of being. It is self-consciousness, not consciousness. On this view, the brain becomes the instrument of the mind and not its creator. Yet it *is* a dimension of our 'bodiliness', and, as such, constitutes a significant aspect of our psychosomatic wholeness or selfhood. We shall see later that this has significant implications for the nature of survival.

So long as the only kind of acceptable evidence is confined to definite facts of sense perception, there is 'no evidence' for the survival of personality beyond death. What is observable provides no sure basis, yet there are constant and uniform aspects of human experience which offer some foundation. The human person has aspirations and also possibilities which the narrow scope of earthly existence cannot satisfy or fulfill. Such unrealized hopes, thwarted ambitions, unsatisfied abilities and unfulfilled capacities provide the themes endlessly in the world's literature and point man beyond this earthly level of existence. Cramped and chained like a bird in a cage, man has stretched longing hands to some larger life beyond. Cried W. Rhodes, "So little done, so much to do." Still more significantly there are arguments for survival which attack and destroy the naturalistic hypothesis and which have at least proved convincing to some of the world's great thinkers from Plato to Kant.

Before we elaborate such arguments, we need to remember that other great thinkers and some religions do not accept personal survival, despite a belief in the reality of God. Thus Spinoza taught that the individual is only a part or 'mode' of the one substance. God is the sole reality. On this pantheistic basis, personal identity ceases at death, but the existence continues, for since it is a mode of the one substance it cannot be destroyed. The spirit is lost in God as the river in the sea. Hegel, as we have already seen, postulated a monism in which individual persons are adjectival existences of the Absolute Spirit. In them, the Absolute is realizing itself through the dialectic of the historical process. Since they are manifestations of the One Spirit, their function is to serve this purpose of self-determination, make their contribution to the life of the Absolute, and then cease to be as personal identities. They are taken up into the forward movement of the Absolute Spirit, and their continued existence is absorption in the life of God. We find the same thought occurring in process thinkers like A. N. Whitehead and Charles Hartshone. For them, personal immortality is replaced by remembered experiences stored up in the developing life of God. The individual attains what they call 'objective immortality' as he contributes to the continually enriched life of the divine being. Beyond death is existence as a memory in God's growing experience. It is interesting to note the Hegelian influence in this more recent philosophical school. Also it needs to be emphasized that many process thinkers like John Cobb are seeking to retain an emphasis on personal survival, difficult as this is in a philosophy which basically is not very hospitable to a genuine continuing personal identity.

We find similar ideas in religions which emphasize mysticism and verge on pantheism. Thus Hinduism in its many forms manifests, in the contemporary scene, a tendency to regard individual destiny as to be merged ultimately in the Brahman, the One. The same emphasis can be found in some forms of Buddhism and in Taoism.

We must now turn to the so-called arguments for personal survival. As with the arguments for divine existence, such arguments are pointers, not convincing proofs. Their value lies perhaps in their cumulative effect. They do at least provide some measure of rational support for the affirmation of faith.

The first argument is based upon the widespread desire of the human race for life beyond death. History manifests a continuing experience of such feelings. Primitive peoples show a marked persistence in the feeling that the dead are somehow still alive and active. Burial was accompanied by the accessories and accouterments that might be needed in the life to come. As thought developed, the idea of survival as ghosts, with the shadowy and vague existence in the Greek Hades or the Hebrew Sheol, took on a deeper significance. Mystery religions arose in the Greek world which took a practical interest in the destiny of the soul and which promised eternal life. Egyptian culture thought much about the destiny of the soul in the land beyond the grave. The ethical aspect of such survival came to the fore. The soul was punished or rewarded in the world-to-come for deeds done in the body. The god of the spirit world was Osiris. He heard the appeal of each soul and passed his judgment upon the plea. The soul pleaded that he had not acted deceitfully, not done evil to men, not oppressed the poor, not judged unjustly, not known ought of wicked things, not committed sin. In Christianity such moral and spiritual implications of the desire for survival find full and complete expression in the promise of an eternal life which may already be experienced within this earthly existence.

All this gives religious and ethical expression to the desires expressed by all peoples in burial sites, on gravestones, in pitiful prayers and written expressions of grief. There is the persistent appeal to human affection, the cry that the tender ties and loving relationships surrendered by death must somehow be renewed in a world beyond. Such persistent desires give some degree of authority to what might seem to be the product of wishful thinking and futile longings. If man is not capable of transcending this earthly life, why this recurring hope of a destiny beyond the world?

This emphasis upon a recurrent desire is sometimes countered by skeptics on the ground that even our physical hungers such as the desire for food are not necessarily met or, still more logically, that at such a level there is always a physical counterpart to match the desire even though that desire may not be satisfied at a particular moment. To arguments like this, we need to point out that such desires as hunger and sex exist because there are actual counterparts by which they can be satisfied. Every physical desire is matched by some aspect of the social and natural environment. Can spiritual desires, such as that for immortality, have no corresponding reality? Does our environment have to be confined to the physical and empirically observable? The scientific method assumes that our intellectual powers will enable us to find the truth about nature. It is this desire, this heuristic passion, for truth which launches the scientist on his quest. Even the naturalist shares in this desire and quest, insofar as he is a scientist. This desire for truth has its objective counterpart. Yet the skeptic denies to feelings and volitions the same validity as he grants to intellectual pursuits and powers. To claim that the intellectual powers are capable of attaining reality but that our moral experience and spiritual feelings and desires have no corresponding objective counterpart is to fall into two errors. The first is the denial of the unity of the human consciousness of which we are increasingly aware. Feelings, desires, volitions are all intimately bound up with the rational aspect of the human mind. We cannot indiscriminately deny validity to some and claim validity for others. Our trust in our intellectual powers is called in question if we deny objective validity to our moral judgments and spiritual desires. The second error is the rationality of the universe. If the universe does not respond to our moral valuations and our spiritual feelings why should it respond to our rational quests?

For the theist there is, of course, another reason. We claim that God is both moral and rational, fully personal where we are imperfectly so. But if he allows us to have desires, like that for immortality, which have no validity, he would be neither moral nor rational. He would be inferior to his creatures, for he would be encouraging us in futile hopes and false expectations.

The second argument is concerned with the incompleteness of earthly existence. It has been called the teleological argument for human survival. Human beings never attain their full potential. There are capacities which are never fulfilled, powers that are never fully actualized. At the spiritual level, new horizons continually open before us and the possibilities of richer developments of spiritual life and perception seem inexhaustible. At the animal and physical level there is frustration and incompleteness. It is, however, at the rational, moral and spiritual levels of human life that incompleteness is most evident. Man is an amphibian, able to transcend his earthly environment and very aware of spiritual values which point beyond this earthly sphere. Such spiritual values have little to do with biological survival. They point to new horizons which cannot be fully reached within earthly existence. They open up possibilities of richer developments in spiritual life and perception which seem inexhaustible and yet to which this world will not permit full realization. To attain full personal being requires a larger sphere beyond earthly existence. Our capacity to transcend our earthly environment and to pursue absolute values requires a future transcendence in which we survive our earthly life.

The third argument is closely akin to the second but places its emphasis on the moral aspect of human existence. Suffering, pain and trouble seem the lot of man, with little or no relation to his moral condition. Injustice and inequity are present in the distribution of life's ills. Evil living does not always receive its just deserts, and virtue is not always rewarded with success and happiness. There must be some future life in which such inequities are put right. The condition for this is, of course, that the universe is a rational whole and has a moral structure. If such a possibility of final readjustment is not postulated, the universe cannot be moral. This is tantamount to believing that there is a personal God who is essentially a moral being. In both the *Republic* and the *Phaedo* Plato stresses this aspect.

In the modern period the same emphasis was made by Kant. He felt that the disparity between holiness and happiness in this life was such that there must be an after-life in which the two were commensurate. In this life the highest good, which is compounded of virtue and happiness, is not attained. Survival beyond death can alone make possible such attainment. For Kant this also requires the existence of a moral God as guarantee that such a state of affairs shall be actualized. Thus the existence of God and personal survival beyond death are closely linked together. Without them there cannot be a world which is both fully rational and ultimately moral.

The fourth argument turns upon the value of personal being. This argument really turns upon a belief in God, for values are absolute only when we believe them to be transcendent, grounded in God and fully actualized in him. There are two aspects of value involved in this argument. First, there is our value to God. As the final creative product of a God of love, the crown of the creative process, man believes himself to be of value to God. But since God is the conserver of values, he will not destroy what he values. He will not allow what he values to perish. Hence the personal being must survive death. Furthermore, personality is bound up with an individuality which gives it a uniqueness possessed by nothing else. Such individuality is, indeed, the basis of love and of man's value. Hence survival cannot mean the expansion of individual selfhood into the impersonal, as held by Hegel and others. Such survival does not preserve personal values.

There is another aspect of value involved—our own valuation in the ideal of a life triumphant over death. If a moral God has allowed us to treasure such an ideal, we cannot believe that he would let us be misled. So once more we come to a pointer towards survival.

All such arguments turn upon a basic presupposition—faith in a moral God and in the rationality at the heart of things. At the best, they point. They certainly do not convince. In addition, the absence of direct evidence makes personal survival a faith-affirmation, a postulate grounded in our religious faith.

There is one area where some thinkers are seeking for evidential support—the area of parapsychology and extra-sensory perception (ESP). In the light of the experiments of J. B. Rhine and others, telepathic communication is, at least, a possibility. Such experiments have demonstrated that the coincidence of the same thought in two minds separated and remote from one another is far higher than statistical calculations based on chance would allow us to expect. It would seem that some factor other than chance is operative, and thus telepathic communication is a real possibility. We note that, in these investigations, such communication between minds does not appear to be weakened by distance. We can find no evidence of physically transmitted waves, of cerebral receivers or transmitters. We seem to be dealing with an occurrence which is purely mental. It has been suggested that there is a common unconscious underlying all minds, rather like Jung's racial unconscious, and that communication takes place at the unconscious level through this mental medium. It may well be that, at this common level, we are unconsciously influencing one another. Furthermore, we may also get in tune in such a medium, despite physical separation, because of a common interest or experience.

The bearing of ESP upon personal survival arises at the level of psychic phenomena. So much trickery has been manifested in this area that we have to tread carefully. The materializations of spirit and associated phenomena are especially open to question, as the Society for Psychical Research has often indicated. What does seem to be established is the authenticity of communication through mediums, despite the presence of fraud. Mediums claim, in a trance, to communicate with the dead, and their messages do pass the judgment of those who consult them as authentic. They do convey private information about personal characteristics and intimate experiences known only to the departed and the client of the medium.

Here, however, we must beware of attributing such messages to those who have died but still exist in some other dimension. Telepathy is a reminder that the medium may be attuned to the mind and personal peculiarities of the departed which are either in the consciousness or deep in the unconscious memory of the client. Various experiments have been performed with mediums which seem to confirm this judgment. Clients have gone to a medium inquiring about a purely fictitious character whom they have invented and received messages portraying this imaginary being as already imagined in the client's mind. Even persons still alive have been portrayed accurately by mediums when consulted by researchers who knowingly have represented such a person as dead. We can only deduce that telepathic communication has been functioning in such cases. Evidently too much store must not be placed by such phenomena.

More recently we have had people who have temporarily died but have been restored to life. Their recorded experiences might suggest movement into another and wider dimension, but here the element of hallucination must not be discounted.

On the balance, we have to turn to the affirmation of religious faith with what support any rational substructure may provide. What then do we mean by personal survival? We have rejected the Greek idea of the soul and its advocates in Christian theology and theistic idealism. The body is no prison house for the soul, as Plato believed, nor is it an appendage which is not finally necessary. The Hebrew idea of the soul as the self in all its totality and complexity, in its psychosomatic wholeness, we have found much more satisfying and akin to our contemporary understanding of man. The body is an intimate and significant part of human personality. Body and mind are intimately bound together in the personal whole, and the 'I', the spirit, is the integrating center of personality. Man's "bodiliness" is the sign of his individuality, and his body is essential to the expression of his personal being. That bodiliness is the outward aspect of his 'I-ness'.

In the light of this, it is easy to understand why the biblical writers used the image of the resurrection of the body rather than that of the immortality of the soul to describe their understanding of personal survival. When theism does not fall into an idealistic trap and retains some degree of realism, it has retained this differentiation. Certainly our previous discussion of man would lead us to speak of the resurrection of the personal whole.

A pluralistic form of theism might suggest one way of understanding such an understanding of survival. In this form, the human body is envisaged as a colony of monads at various levels of consciousness organically related to one another and integrated around a central monad, the inner soul and spirit. Thus energy, which appears to be physical, is actually mental in essence. At death, the central monad gathers around itself a new structure of monads which provide a new and more adequate bodiliness for the new dimension of being into which the person enters.

Such an explanation involves a special ontology which is acceptable to thinkers as diverse as H. H. Farmer and the process thinkers. Since we do not know what energy itself is, we might meet the situation more simply by picturing a transformation of bodiliness into a form of energy more appropriate to and adequate for the larger and more spiritual existence into which the theist believes that persons are ushered on death. What is clear is that some new form of bodiliness would seem to be required if personal identity and fellowship by communication are to be essential characteristics in that new order. A monistic absorption in the One, such as Hegel envisaged, or a mystical absorption into God, such as forms of pantheism and Hinduism offer can only be avoided if personal individuality and unity in fellowship are preserved. For such individualization with communication some form of bodiliness and concomitant separation would seem essential. Whatever form energy may take in such a new bodiliness is beyond our imagining.

One last point must be made. Resurrection is God's act. We cannot speak of natural immortality, but rather of a divine act of reconstitution in which the original personal being now appears in a new dimension with a new bodiliness. This raises issues for the theist about divine judgment and the destiny of the wicked. Here we tend to move into theology proper and must come to rest in the grace of God fully manifested in Jesus Christ. Philosophical thinking gives place to theological concern with a special revelation. We still, however, have to face the issue of evil in this world and the challenge which it presents to a theistic understanding of the universe.

Theism's Most Crucial Challenge— The Mystery of Evil

7 We must now face the issue which can shake our confidence in the theistic approach to ultimate reality. One potent fact in human experience is the reality of evil in its many forms. It raises questions about the theistic understanding of God as good and as omnipotent. The shadow cast by the mystery of evil tends to darken the idea of divine goodness and to challenge God's omnipotence. Either God is good and not all-powerful. Or God is all-powerful and not good. Evil has one aspect, moral evil, which is completely bound up with man's freedom. We have seen that this is mystery enough from the point of view of the scientific approach to nature. It is still more so when we consider its place in a theistic universe. What does human freedom mean to God and how is it related to the divine omnipotence? Is human freedom really an illusion and are divine predestination and divinely directed determinism the true picture of man's place in God's world? If freedom is a reality, it sets limits on God's omnipotence and the goodness of his creation. For this reason, theism often totters on the edge of human determinism. But then natural evil, the other aspect of evil, with its contingencies, its suffering, its untoward circumstances and its calamitous occurences raises other issues for religious faith. How can a good and loving God create and sustain a world which is "red in tooth and claw with ravine"? How can we explain human suffering and undeserved trouble in a theistic world? So the issue of

theodicy, of the justification of God, raises its head on every side.

The issue of evil arises with the awareness of absolute values—happiness, beauty, truth and goodness. In a perfect world. devised by a good God, we might expect that all such values would be present and actualized. But we also find their opposites—pain, ugliness, error and moral evil, respectively. The issues of error and ugliness do not come within the purview of our theme. What concern us here are the negative aspects of happiness and moral virtue—pain and sin.

Moral and Natural Evil

The usual description of the physical ills which beset humankind is natural evil. This covers the whole gamut from physical disasters like earthquakes, floods and whirlwinds to physiological diseases and psychological maladies like cancers and psychoses. Pain, suffering and death describe the subjective dimensions of such natural ills. Our Victorian forbears were very conscious of the cruel sufferings and ravages which the struggle for existence brought to the animal order. Tennyson celebrated it in his poem "In Memoriam" and could describe nature as "red in tooth and claw with ravine." For him there was also the terrible wastage of nature—"out of fifty seeds," nature "brings but one to bear." So climbing the world's great altar stairs of sacrifice, he falters and doubts. Darwin's understanding of the evolutionary process as a struggle for existence in which only the fittest survived led his great disciple T. H. Huxley to speak of nature as a 'dismal cockpit'. John Stuart Mill could voice the feelings of many of his contemporaries when he wrote: "In sober truth, nearly all the things for which men are hanged or imprisoned for doing to one another are nature's everyday performances." Nature takes both life itself and the means by which life is sustained, in particular human life. Hurricanes, locusts, earthquakes, chemical changes in edible roots all bring dire consequences for human beings. At every level, life involves sensitivity to pain, and every form of organic life carries in itself the seeds of its final dissolution. Nature itself produces the bacilli, the misdirected growths, the misshapen structures which occur throughout the range of living things. It equips creatures with natural weapons for preying on other creatures. Indeed, the well-being of the higher orders of creation, including man himself, depends for food upon the suffering and death of other forms of life.

Sensitivity to animal suffering may often be sentimental. We cannot, however, take refuge under such a label when we turn to man himself. Earthquakes, volcanic eruptions, tidal waves, hurricanes, floods and tornadoes take their toll of the human race. And mere private ills like poverty, hunger, disease and mental illness bring pain and suffering to many. Finally, the grim specter of death and its attendant grief and bereavement loom up before all men. No wonder that Horace Walpole could suggest that "life is a comedy to those who think, a tragedy to those who feel."

For a materialistic or naturalistic thinker such evils are real but they do not raise the problems which arise in the mind of the religious person. For one like the theist who believes in a moral God and holds to a divine goodness as the substructure of the universe, the natural evils of the world present a moral challenge. They are an indictment of the moral structure of the universe. They present no pattern of justice or equity. Ills come to all alike, irrespective of their moral status or spiritual attitude. Adversity and trouble are no selectors of persons. Virtue does not connote happiness. Integrity of character and deep religious commitment have little relation to either prosperity or adversity. The wicked often flourish like the green bay tree, and the righteous are overwhelmed by trouble. Death is no chooser of persons. It seems indifferent to intellectual gifts, moral integrity, and social usefulness. To believe in the goodness and power of God is no easy thing in our world. Shakespeare was a cynic, but he touched the bone for many when he wrote that "life is a tale told by an idiot, full of sound and fury, signifying nothing."

Yet many of the ills which men suffer result from society. Man's social environment is a major cause of human trouble, adversity and suffering. Indeed, of his two environments, social and natural, the former seems to loom large, especially today. This immediately turns our eyes to the issue of human freedom and the reality of moral evil. Man's inhumanity to man, the oppression and tyranny which lift their heads in every human society, the prevalence of human depravity, selfish acquisitiveness, personal arrogance, anti-social wrongdoing, and corporate greed—all are indications of the place of the human will as a major source of evil. The naturalist may explain it all as an aspect of the struggle for survival. But, for the theist, it raises issues more deep-seated than do the physical and natural ills that beset the human race.

Because of his natural heritage, man has the same instincts and impulses as the animal order. Sex, hunger, aggressiveness, self-preservation are powerful forces deep down in his unconscious, and they make themselves felt in his conscious life. Furthermore, the whole evolutionary process has been directed towards the structuring of individual selves within which individual freedom and personal self-awareness can become a reality. Now such a movement towards selfhood means a tendency for all the biological forces of the organism to become centered, despite the opposite tendency towards group life and the mergence of the individual within its specific social milieu. Self-preservation is a powerful force in the development of the species. The Darwinian formula of 'the struggle for survival' is a reminder of this. When man emerges with the 'miracle' of freedom, all these tendencies are present with the pains attendant on their unfulfillment. If he voluntarily chooses to satisfy his impulses irrespective of any concern for his fellows, to reject the call of interpersonal responsibility and to choose his own selfish satisfaction, moral evil results. Thus man's natural heritage provides the raw material which, conjoined to his capacity for free choice, leads to sin. The impulse to self-preservation, when man chooses to satisfy it, irrespective of the needs and condition of his fellows, results in moral evil and social ill.

Society has always imposed a limit on such behavior and set a norm to which its members are required to conform. The roots of this lie back in the sub-human groups, as we have already noted. The theist would see such moral and social laws as within the divine will and as manifestations of the creative direction of the life processes by the Creator. To deviate from the norm and to choose the self provides the definition for moral evil. Sin is self-will. It converts the impulse for self-preservation into moral selfishness. Moral evil and social order thus belong together. Directly Robinson Crusoe finds Man Friday, some kind of ordering appears by which relationships are directed. And since man has been social from his very genesis, such social structuring, with its moral import, has always been present in human life. The outward pressure of the social norm has been matched by the inward moral consciousness. Freedom carries within itself moral responsibility. Man cannot allow his natural drives to be satisfied irresponsibly. They must be harnessed to responsible choice. He is a rational being with the power to decide how he shall direct his power, including that vital urge to self-preservation. Moral evil results from a voluntary choice by a rational being against the ordered structure of personal relationships in which his life is set.

We have suggested that the moral dimension is an innate part of man's personal structure from his very genesis. Undoubtedly the moral norm was first experienced in the form of tribal custom or *mores* with accompanying *tabus*. In this way man's moral consciousness was educated and man's social structures were developed until the full dimensions of man's moral being could become effective. What is essential to any understanding of moral evil is man's rational nature and his freedom, his ability for rational and voluntary choice. These would appear to be present from the beginning. Furthermore, the presence of religion in the tribal life meant that the *mores* and their accompanying *tabus* were placed under the guardianship of the deity. The dawning of moral evil in the human consciousness thus took on the coloring of sin.

Man's moral evil moves across the surface of society like ripples across the surface of a pond. Social evil is the result of human wrong-doing. Aggressiveness and selfish self-preservation bring the attendant ills of acquisitiveness, oppression, tyranny, poverty, war and death for many others. Moral evil thus becomes a collective force, reinforced by an aggregation of evil wills and spreading its tentacles throughout the social structure. It can become corporate, embodied in the state, in economic interests, in political groupings. Suffering, pain, death can attend its way. Not only so, but such evil can create a social environment in which succeeding generations are subjected to its influences. Thereby moral evil is propagated down the movement of history as well as across the spread of society.

Once more the theist faces issues which challenge his faith in the goodness and power of God. Why does evil flourish? Why do the innocent suffer and the wicked prosper? On every hand questions are raised, and evil becomes a crucial challenge to any religious faith and especially to theism.

Metaphysical Issues and Solutions

Already we are pointing to the metaphysical problems which the forms of evil present to religious faith. We, too, ask why evil exists at all in the world and whether it is accidental or necessary. Behind any attempt to answer such questions is the deeper one of the nature of God and his relation to the evil in the world.

Four solutions have been offered to issues like this. The first is that of *pessimism* which frankly denies the goodness of God and regards the world as positively and fundamentally evil. The second is the *dualistic* solution. Here a principle of evil is postulated *pari passu* a principle of good. This evil god is responsible for all moral and natural evil, and thus the moral nature of the good God is not impugned. The third solution is the *optimistic* one which regards all evil in its forms as subordinate to, and serving the ends of, a good God and his moral purpose.

The fourth solution is the *melioristic* one. This accepts the reality of evil as a positive force and regards certain aspects of its presence and activity as shrouded in mystery. Yet it believes that, on the balance, there is sufficient indication of goodness in the world to confirm religious faith in a moral God. Evil is not sufficiently strong to contradict the affirmations of such faith and to make belief in the moral structure of the universe impossible. A religious interpretation of the facts is possible which brings goodness uppermost. Frequently this solution is bound up with an *eschatological* viewpoint, which could be offered as an appended solution. In this case, goodness will triumph in the end and evil will be vanquished. God will triumph at the end of history. Very often this viewpoint is appended also to the dualistic solution. The melioristic solution, with or without an eschatological addendum, does not offer a watertight and rigorously logical solution. But then evil is a mystery to be lived with by faith and not a problem to be solved by logic. All we can do is hope that religious faith will grant us sufficient insight into the depths of the mystery for such a faith to be confirmed. This is what the melioristic solution attempts to do.

Particularly in the case of theism, such attempts to offer a justification of God have been termed theodicy. First coined by Leibnitz, this term was used to describe an optimistic justification of theistic faith. Actually theism has employed each of the last three solutions, together with the eschatological addendum, and we must examine such attempts. Before we do this, however, we must examine other attempts to deal with the relation of evil to religious views of God which are not theistic.

The pessimistic solution is not necessarily irreligious. Indeed, the Eastern religions of Hinduism and Buddhism fall under this classification. Such religions are world-denying and regard life in the world as a recurrent cycle of existence from which men need to be redeemed. In the basic form of Hinduism, Brahmanism, man's soul is basically identified with the deity. His breath-soul, Atman, is Brahman, and salvation comes in the recognition of this identity with its attendant mystical absorption. Human existence in this world consists of continuing cycles of birth and death, in which the soul is continually reincarnated, until, at last, deliverance comes and it is united with the One. These recurrent cycles of existence constitute *samsara*, and the judgment or *Karma* upon the life so lived determines the next cycle of existence. Because the soul is identical with Brahman, this world is *maya*, illusion. Existence in the world is futile. It accomplishes nothing. God or Brahman is beyond good and evil, the sole reality.

Buddhism, in its form of Hinayana or Theravada, is virtually atheism. It seems to deny the reality of God unless it so defines nothingness or Nirvana. It certainly denies personal identity and the reality of the soul. All it retains from Hinduism is the recurrent cycles of Samsara/Karma through which the bundle of desires which constitute man are finally suppressed. The major evil is suffering and its cause is desire. When that desire is extinguished, suffering is also extinguished, and Nirvana or nothingness is attained. Existence ceases.

Neither of these religions offers an explanation of evil. Both offer a practical way of escape—either mystical contemplation, with its accompanying techniques, or the noble eightfold path of Gautama Buddha.

Leibnitz first drew marked attention to the metaphysical basis of evil. We may describe this as metaphysical evil. It is the necessary imperfection of the finite and created. From it results natural or physical evil, and closely bound up with it is the imperfection of finite creatures endowed with freedom and yet limited by their finitude in knowledge and experience. We shall return to this later. Here we need to note that both the religions just discussed, by denying creation and the reality of the creaturely order, avoid the possibility of metaphysical evil with the attendant physical and moral forms of evil.

In a much more physical vein, we have a thoroughgoing pessimism in the pantheistic system of Schopenhauer. For him ultimate reality is blind, irrational will. Like Gautama, he was obsessed with human suffering. In consequence he attacked optimism as a bitter mockery of mankind's unspeakable suffering. For him there could be no personal God, no directing purpose or overruling wisdom in the process. Reality was an unconscious and irrational universal will. This surging will was progressively objectifying itself in individual persons and things. It was manifest in human psychology by endless and never satisfied desire. Schopenhauer regarded intelligence or knowlege as purely secondary. He saw it as an aid to the individual organism in its struggle to subsist and propagate its kind. Indeed, he pictured the relation of intelligence to will as that of a lame man perched upon the shoulders of a blind man and directing his movements. By so regarding intelligence and thought as secondary and purely utilitarian, he produced a pessimistic philosophy in which all was empty and aimless striving. His pantheistic approach saw this aimless striving universally present in all men. They are dominated by a succession of desires which can never be satisfied. Yet men, despite the futility of trying, are driven on by a search for happiness only to find it hollow and unsatisfying. Evil will becomes the sole reality, present in all men as desire.

Buddha also saw desire as the root of evil, but he was activated by compassion and pity for humanity. Schopenhauer was a cynical pessimist, contemptuous of life and of the men who lived it. His condemnation of desire ignores the manifest fact that desire is the root of good as well as of evil. Aspiration and endeavor constitute life's greatness and goodness. Hope and desire for happiness cannot be summarily dismissed. Because they do lure us on to greater endeavor, they bring achievements and goods which at least counterbalance and more probably outweigh the evils attendant upon some human desires.

The later developments of Schopenhauer's thought retain the somber pessimism, yet they do stress asceticism as an escape from the suffering inherent in blind surging will in all its manifestations as individual desire. The holiness of the ascetic should lead to permanent redemption from the suffering of the world. Here Schopenhauer advocates aesthetic contemplation and links with it ethical discernment. For him this should make redemption possible by leading to a denial of the will to live. Akin to Buddhism!

The direct opposite of such pessimism is the optimistic stance adopted by both pantheists and panentheistic monists. We shall reserve until the next section a treatment of theists like Leibnitz who adopted an optimistic viewpoint. Here we shall confine ourselves to non-theistic philosophies. Such monisms reject divine transcendence and emphasize immanence. In addition, they have an ontological base in which finite beings participate in and are manifestations of the divine ground of being. Finally, they seek, because of this, to produce a self-consistent system which has no room in it for the reality of evil. Hence we have a denial of the real existence of evil. *Sub specie aeternitatis*—under the aspect of eternity—all forms of evil are nonexistent. Ultimate reality is perfect goodness. Whatever exists participates in that reality and is good. Therefore finally all evil, moral and physical, subserves a higher good and is illusory.

Spinoza defined God as the one all-embracing infinite Substance. This perfect whole is beyond good and evil. It embraces within itself the two parallel attributes of extension and thought within which, respectively, individual bodies and minds are modes of existence. This pantheism thus posits the world as divine and regards sin and evil as negations.

Hegel's approach is more panentheistic than pantheistic. His monism identifies ultimate reality with one absolute Mind or Spirit. The world becomes this One Spirit moving towards rational self-determination. The world is its reasoning process or dialectic. The Spirit objectivizes itself in nature and society and subjectivizes itself in individual persons. Thereby the progressive dialectic of opposites, subjects and objects, moves toward the continuing rational enrichment of the Absolute. Individuals are adjectival existents, transient manifestations of the One Spirit as it moves to self-realization. All is therefore within the Whole, the One, and that Whole is rational. In consequence, sin and physical evil can have no final reality. They exist within the dialectical movement only as necessary phases in the self-realization of the Absolute. What we have called metaphysical evil is also transient and not finally real, since all finite beings are reabsorbed in the One, to whose rational development they make their contribution. From the point of view of the whole, evil is unreal and disappears. It exists only from the partial point of view available from within the process.

Bradley, a later disciple of Hegel, follows a similar line. He regards sin as a discord which disappears if the appearance is made wide enough (*Appearance and Reality*, p. 202). Likewise, Bosanquet can describe evil as good in the wrong place, so that there is nothing in evil which cannot be absorbed in good and be contributory to it. (*The Value and Destiny of the Individual*, pp. 209ff.).

This optimistic standpoint makes sin purely negative and does not give it the positive reality which is so evident in actual existence. Indeed, sin is even made to serve a purpose within the progressive development of the Absolute Spirit. It becomes a necessary stage in the movement towards a higher good. This would appear to suggest that the path to virtue is through sin. What is logically satisfactory is not, however, existentially true. If we believe that individual persons are real and of value in their own right, we cannot regard sin and evil so lightly. So long as individuals have merely transient actuality and serve the purpose of the whole, we can treat even their sin as serving the higher good of the whole. If, however, they are of value in themselves, their indulgence in sin makes no contribution to their individual good. Rather, it tends to destroy them. Furthermore, such indulgence is of no benefit to their immediate neighbors or society. Sin is a positive and destructive force, and it is certainly not a necessary stage in the movement to harmonious wholeness in the universe, except for these who dwell in 'the cloud-cuckoo land' of monistic idealism.

One contribution that such monism makes, however, is to link up evil in all its forms with the development of the universe. This connection is very evident in the humanistic cult of progress, which has flourished in certain periods of this century and still periodically lifts its head. This is a cult of human perfectibility. Largely under the influence of the evolutionary ideas which have become biological orthodoxy, it has viewed the process of human history in developmental and progressive terms. Often it has identified sin with ignorance and argued that education and social planning will finally be sufficient to eliminate errant human behavior. To this is added the progress of modern science and its technological achievement. These are regarded as sufficient ultimately to control both the evils arising from the natural environment and, at the medical level, the diseases, with their attendant suffering, which affect man's bodily and mental states. Faced frequently by the disillusionment arising from wars and economic greed, such humanism still lifts its head and produces ecological and educational idealists who, though not believing in God, still believe in human nature.

The third approach to the mystery of evil is that of dualism. Early religions like Manicheism which regarded matter, including the human body, as evil have long since vanished. Zoroastrianism is, however, a more viable dualism and still has its devotees in Iran and also among the Parsees in India. It regards the world as the scene of a struggle between two supernatural powers and their attendant spirits, Ahura Mazda (Ormazd), the good god, and Angra Mainyu (Ahriman), the evil deity. Life itself is a constant conflict between the powers of good and evil. In the present conflict, religion and morality alike require men to take sides for the good against the evil powers. Zoroastor himself seems to have regarded this dualism as a limited one, since, for him, Ahura Mazda was finally supreme and Angra Mainyu was subordinate to him. Later Zoroastrianism seems to have been more thoroughgoing in its dualism, but it too found an eschatological solution. In the end the good God would triumph over evil.

Zoroastrianism eventually moves towards a theistic position and merges into a form of meliorism with its eschatological emphasis. It has contributed its elaborate angelology to biblical thinking and reinforced thereby the late biblical idea of the devil. In this way, we can find a limited dualism in some forms of Christian theology, again resolved by an eschatological emphasis.

This brings us to near-theistic and theistic attempts to deal with the mystery of evil.

Panentheism and Radical Monotheism Face the Challenge

We have already indicated that optimism and dualism find a place in theistic thought about evil but some form of meliorism provides the best answer.

We may begin by looking at Leibnitz, whose philosophy we have already referred to and whose emphasis on metaphysical evil has already been noted. Leibnitz held to a theistic position in which God is regarded as creator and sustainer of the world. As such, God could conceive many different world structures, but our world was the only one that it was possible for him to actualize by his creative fiat. In creating a world of finite beings, God limited himself. For, although omnipotent and infinite, he could not transfer his mind and will to the finite without limitation. Thus metaphysical evil was a necessary accompaniment of the creative act. What is created and finite is necessary imperfect. God could not transfer his own perfection to his creatures. The imperfections in the world are not created by God. They are due to the fact that the creaturely nature is "incapable of being without limits" (to use Leibnitz's own words—*Monadology*, Latta's translation, p. 240).

This metaphysical evil gave rise both to physical or natural evil and to sin or moral evil. At the physical level, nature consists of a whole series of monads or mental entities at various levels of unconsciousness and consciousness. Their lack of perfection has a privative effect so that some evil arises from imperfection. But evil also comes in the form of pain and suffering because of the interaction of the monads with one another, also shot through with the lack of perfection. At the level of man, the central monad or soul is endowed with freedom. It is, however, limited in both knowledge and experience so that man misdirects his freedom and behaves himself imperfectly by disobedience to both God and man. From this abuse of freedom arise sin and moral evil.

Despite the presence of evil in its many forms and the necessity of metaphysical evil, Leibnitz asserted that this was 'the best of all possible worlds'. The evils are relatively small, and Leibnitz compares them to the discords by the presence of which the aesthetic value of a musical movement is enhanced. Physical evils like pain are necessarily implied in a world of finite beings, while Leibnitz tends to reduce the abuse of freedom to the limitation implicit in metaphysical evil.

Furthermore, God is unceasingly active in his creation, producing a growing good. So Leibnitz sounds the eschatological note. Ultimately all the evils will be seen to fit into God's benevolent plan. This plan, however, is already in God's mind as a pre-established harmony. And it is here that we face the rigorous pluralism of Leibnitz. He can describe the monads as windowless. They act only from within, and not in direct response to what is without. They are, indeed, 'programed' and mirror the whole world within themselves. Thus they are foreordained to act in a way which accords with the pre-established harmony. Their inner world, on Leibnitz's view, is independent of everything else *except God*. The last words account for the unity of the whole. Without such a safeguard the assembly of independent and isolated monads would breed anarchy. But God is active in the world, and the monads are not independent of him. They are related to one another through his mediation, and thereby their interaction, although always from within, is yet in accord with his plan. Through the intervention of this Supreme Monad, the harmony of the whole is preserved, and God's goal will be attained. He is, indeed, the absolute ground of the unity of the world.

Leibnitz did endeavor to maintain a theistic viewpoint and uphold the divine omnipotence while preserving the freedom and individuality of the creatures. His logical argument leads to undue optimism with his belief in "the best of all possible worlds." Yet it also has the seeds of a melioristic position, although it does not take seriously enough the positive aspect of evil. His denial of direct interaction between the monads and his doctrine of a pre-established harmony weaken his position, especially in regard to freedom. Theistic thought, however, has ever since paid attention to his thought.

A much more radical view of evil was held by Immanuel Kant. His theistic position involved him in a high emphasis upon man's moral consciousness. He held that the key to understanding man lay in the ethical categorical imperative. But he was also aware of the sensuous dimension in human nature. Hence, while emphasizing man's consciousness of the moral law, he also recognized that man was subject to sensuous impulses. Both must be taken into account in the understanding of man. Since man's true unity turned upon the will, the normal relation of the moral and the sensuous should be the subordination of the latter to the former. Kant recognized that actually the reverse of this is the case. The sensuous impulses resist moral direction and sway the human will towards evil. Thus man has a natural bent toward evil. Yet man does recognize his responsibility for such radical evil, so that its presence is not necessary.

Kant was aware also of the inequities of life. He recognized that holiness and happiness were often not matched in human existence. Men ought to be holy but they desired happiness, and somehow duty and desire, virtue and happiness did not meet in this life. Because he believed that this is a moral universe, we find him sounding the eschatological note and postulating immortality so that the true balance shall be made in an afterlife. Furthermore, his belief in God partly rested on his assurance that only the existence of a moral God could guarantee such ultimate harmony.

Kant reduces orthodox Christianity to the level of ethical theism, at times almost deism. For him religion consisted, as we saw in the first chapter, in man's regarding his moral imperatives as divine commands. Yet he did recognize the radical nature of moral evil, without moving into the ideas associated with original sin. Also he emphasized the inequities which natural evil visits upon virtue.

The issue which confronts the theist is bound up with how a good God can create a world in which evil in its many forms is a reality. The Boston school endeavored to meet this issue by postulating a limited or finite deity. Thus E. S. Brightman would attribute finitude to God. He believed God to be good and personal, worthy of devotion and the ground of all values. He is creator and sustainer of the universe, and he controls the course of human history. Yet experience shows that there is something in God's nature which makes the effort and pain of life necessary. His reason and active creative will, which constitute his essential being, have therefore to reckon with something in him which makes necessary the shadow side of the created world. Brightman and his followers call this element in God 'the Given'. This word describes non-rational conditions in the divine nature which God's will has not created and of which he does not approve. He struggles with it and maintains a constant and growing control over it. Yet he never completely controls the Given. His will and reason act on the Given to produce the world and to achieve value in it. But just as the Given produces a problem in God so it produces a problem in his world. For it produces the evils of life and the delay in the attainment of values. Thus evil, insofar as it does not result from the misuse of human freedom, is due to God's nature but not wholly to his deliberate choice. He is a limited God, but not limited from without, as dualism would suggest. Rather he is limited from within himself by the Given which constitutes one dimension of his nature. It is a surd quantity which baffles and bewilders his conscious action. Experience itself shows that God attains his purpose gradually through effort, difficulty and suffering. Indeed, God's nature includes suffering, caused by the struggle with and victory over opposition within. This insight is valuable for our later discussion, even though we change its points of reference.

The idea that God's transcendence involves an otherness which accounts for evil occurs also in the approach of Paul Tillich. Brightman does not really account for or describe his Given. Tillich goes back to the insights of the mystic, Jacob Boehme, already used by Schelling. Boehme felt that there was a depth in God, the Abyss, the *Ungrund*. Indeed the *Ungrund* is God as the undifferentiated Absolute, neither light nor darkness, neither love nor wrath, the ineffable. Tillich adopted and adapted this thought, postulating a 'God beyond God'. He pointed to a 'form-destroying' depth in the divine nature which is swallowed up in the divine infinitude. There is present in God's transcendent wholeness a dimension of non-being, the form-destructive element. Thereby Tillich can speak of God's nature as a duality of being and non-being. In consequence his presence in the world is both form-creative and form-destructive. Here Tillich harnesses to his understanding of God Otto's description of the holy as the transcendent mystery which both attracts and repels. God has his terrifying aspect, as well as making himself known as the quintessence of moral perfection. The presence of the abyss of non-being, the form-destroying dimension in God, explains God's dynamic nature. He is both possibility and fulfilment. He both goes forth from himself and rests back upon himself. He creates and reveals himself but this dynamic activity of becoming is balanced by a static aspect of rest.

It is at this point that Tillich, like Brightman, departs from classic theism and moves into panentheism (as we have defined it). Neither of these thinkers accepts the formula *creatio ex nihilo*. In both cases the world is produced by a voluntary creative act from God's own being. The emphasis must fall on the word 'voluntary', for the world does not come by logical necessity as with Hegel. It results from a free creative decision, but there is continuity between it and the ground of its being. Tillich's philosophy is, indeed, a full ontology. There is no irrationality here like 'creation out of nothing', and thus, for him, religion is grounded in a mystical *a priori*. He does, however, maintain a definite distinction between God and his creatures. The reason for this is the presence in them of the form-destructive element, the element of non-being. Although kept subordinate by the infinitude of the divine being, it is released by the finitude of creaturely being. Drawing their being from God, they also have the duality of being and non-being. But their finite status allows non-being to assert itself with its form-destructive powers. Hence evil arises in the created order and specifically, in the case of man, when the negative aspect misdirects and violates his freedom. In a famous sermon entitled "Nature Mourns a Lost Good," Tillich makes it clear that nature and man alike suffer from the presence of the threat of non-being and from the ever-present demonic distortions and perversions which this form-destroying aspect introduces into the created order.

Once more we find ourselves on the edge of Christian orthodoxy and classic theism. Yet there are insights in Tillich's understanding of the dynamic nature of God and of the dialectic state of man and his world, threatened always by non-being and the demonic tendency. He does recognize the reality of metaphysical evil, and he tends to associate sin more with the creative emergence of finitude than with a responsible decision grounded in human freedom. This judgment might be open to debate, although it is difficult to avoid the view that sin is associated with finitude rather than personal choice.

We must now attempt to assess the significance of evil for, and the insights into the mystery of evil offered by, classical theism. We shall, in so doing, consider modifications in the understanding of God which would seem to be required. A melioristic stance would seem to be required. Optimism mocks at the human soul, since the radical and positive presence of evil will not allow any superficial approach. The pessimistic outlook often arises because it is bound up with a hedonistic evaluation of life and regards happiness as life's ideal. Yet even at the level of such an ideal, the deepest joy often comes only against the background of pain. Shelley (in "To a Skylark") saw this when he wrote that:

> Our sincerest laughter
> With some pain is fraught,
> Our sweetest songs are those which tell
>   of saddest thought. . . .

But even then it is highly doubtful whether pure happiness is the free and highest value. Kant was sure that it had its place, but he valued morality much higher, feeling that somehow virtue must ultimately be matched with happiness.

The melioristic approach recognizes ultimate mystery but holds that the balance of goods is sufficient to make theistic faith tenable. Let us examine this at the level of life's physical ills—pain, suffering, death.

The overall directiveness of the evolutionary process, which we have already examined, is also marked by an element of randomness and by contingencies. We have the occurrence of random mutations in the development of the species. We also have the presence of acausality and indeterminacy in atomic phenomena at the basis of matter and energy. Then we are also recognizing that the so-called laws of nature, the regularities which science studies, are statistical averages and describe the average and expected behavior of nature. All this suggests that something like Brightman's Given or Tillich's non-being may be present in the process. Even the biblical writers recognized this, despite their limited knowledge, when they described God as beginnning with chaos, deep, darkness, a formless void in the creation of the world. (Gen. 1). This suggests that God began with chaos and shaped it into cosmos, a point of view which the big-bang theory of the origin of the universe also supports. The evolutionary process and the movement of human history point to this being an unfinished universe, a world in the making, in which the creative Presence is still at work.

This need not mean the panentheistic approaches of Brightman and Tillich. Rather we may take the point of view that God called a chaos into being because this best served the ultimate fulfilment of his purpose. Here, indeed, we may listen to Leibnitz while rejecting his undue optimism with its pre-established harmony. In this way, God produced a developing universe in which there was flexibility and not rigid determinism. As we have already suggested, what appeared to be physical energy had within it the potencies for life, mind and ultimately self-conscious mind or Spirit. Moreover, we may see certain habitual forms of behavior ingredient in the energy and becoming evident at the various levels of complexity into which the energy was patterned as the process proceeded. As the process developed under the creative direction of the Creator, we find both a growing structure with certain regularities of behavior and also a flexibility which left possibilities for development open. In this way, on our planet, a world was being shaped with sufficient openness and unfinishedness for free and creative human beings to live in and operate when they emerged. If God's plan was to produce free creators, rational beings able to cooperate with him in completing his purpose, then we can glimpse some meaning in the physical or natural evils which have attended man's historical existence. They result from the unfinished nature of the universe and the flexibility introduced into it by the Creator. We cannot say that this was the best way God could fulfill his purpose, for at the best we can but dimly grasp his creative mind. But we may say that the world is open and unfinished in order that it may serve his purpose in the coming of man and his freedom. And we can see some reasons for this.

If our presentation of the world be correct we can at least give some justification for and explanation of natural evil. There are, for instance, those ills which result from the regularities or uniformities without which no ongoing structured universe would be possible. Such so-called laws like gravitation do often bring suffering in the train of their operation. Again, the development of life itself and the emergence of higher and more complex levels of organisms would seem to require warring systems. Life grows by challenge and response, and the new seems to require changes in the environment which bring suffering in their wake. Further, such warring systems, with the constitutive laws and uniformities, often harness the chaotic and unfinished aspects of the universe, thereby increasing the ill effects of their presence. We think of wind storms, floods, and earthquakes, of disease germs and abnormal cell growths like cancers. Here we are touching the mysterious depths of evil.

While it is true that pain can become the spur to endeavor and suffering may lead to self-development, this is but a frail justification for the abnormal and undeserved suffering and trouble which attend humankind in the kinds of evil just listed. It is true that the struggle for existence brings suffering and hardship, but it may also lead to nobler character and deeper spirituality as well as physical well-being. Yet life brings an overplus of evil which bears little such meaning. There are ills that bear down the soul and which seem to have no significance in the divine purpose. The only lifting of mystery and fringe of justification may lie in the vision of a God who has chosen this way of growing free souls and who is prepared to pay the price himself. Such a vision of God theism must offer. Christ on his Cross may point even theistic philosophy to a vision of a God whose power is that of suffering love, the power of a restraint which respects our freedom, bears our suffering with us, and constrains his world towards the fulfilment of his plan.

When we turn from natural evil to moral evil, we may find the going a little easier. Theism's emphasis on the reality of human freedom and responsibility at least suggests that God's creative purpose involved the possibility of sin and selfishness, vice and pride. There can be no real freedom without the possibility of misdoing, wrong decisions, evil behavior. To be free to do God's will is also to be free to reject it. Only so can moral values be real. Were we just a set of puppets dancing to a divine direction, morality would have no meaning. This, of course, entails responsibility on God's part. Hence again we turn to the reality of divine suffering and the possibility of atoning love. We do not escape this by throwing back responsibility upon a devil. For unless we want to indulge in a thoroughgoing dualism, we are only postulating another and more demonic figure whose fall has resulted from mishandled freedom. Thus we are not evading the final divine responsibility for the creation of free beings.

Moral demands and a moral structure of the universe which makes judgment a reality are not sufficient to set man free from his selfishness and pride. This testimony of human history as well of individual experience bids us beware of optimism. The radical nature of moral evil to which Kant bore testimony will not allow us to adopt a shallow solution. Our animal nature with its impulses and instinctual urges is often too strong for man to control it in the service of moral imperatives and spiritual visions. We cannot escape our selfishness and self-centeredness that easily. Here is the mystery of our being. And only a divine love which suffers with us, bearing our wrongdoings and suffering in its consequences, yet still loving us, can conquer our bondage and set us really free to do his will. But here theistic philosophy can only point, and Christian theology must gather up the strands.

Index